BLACK & WHITE DEVELOPING AND PRINTING

Consultant Editor   Neville Maude

Collins

CONTENTS

Published in 1983 by
William Collins Sons & Co Ltd
London • Glasgow • Sydney •
Auckland • Johannesburg

Designed and produced for
William Collins Sons & Co Ltd
by Eaglemoss Publications Limited

First published in *You and Your Camera*
© 1983 by Eaglemoss Publications Limited

ISBN 0 00 411771 9

Printed in Great Britain

INTRODUCTION

Increasing numbers of photographers are turning to home developing and printing. The reasons are various, but there is no doubt that, besides the saving in costs, there is a great deal of fun to be had in producing your own black and white prints.

Perhaps you are lucky enough to have access to a school or camera club darkroom. If not, this book shows you how to set up your own temporary or permanent darkroom. Essential equipment is described, discussed and illustrated with clear photographs and diagrams. The book guides you through each stage of the developing and printing procedures. Detailed explanations of exactly what to do are accompanied by step-by-step illustrations and numerous examples of the finished result. Pitfalls are pointed out, as well as remedies for any faults in your prints or negatives. Choice of the various processing chemicals and printing papers is dealt with thoroughly. The emphasis is on darkroom safety and efficiency at all times.

Having learnt the basics, you can refine and develop your techniques to achieve black and white prints of a quality far surpassing that of commercial processors. Just follow the sections on making enlargements, retouching and colour toning for an introduction to one of the most fascinating aspects of photography.

The improvised darkroom

Photographers who wish to keep full control over every stage of picture-making will soon find themselves tucked away in some corner at home, engrossed in developing and printing. When space allows, a permanent darkroom is the most satisfactory arrangement but you can still do all kinds of darkroom work in a temporary, improvised set-up. Almost any room can be quickly and easily converted for photographic processing. It must be efficiently blacked out, of course, and there have to be power outlets for the enlarger and safelight, but running water is not essential. Once a film or prints are fixed they can be put in a plastic bucket of water and taken to another room for the important final wash.

Power can be laid on almost anywhere with an appropriate extension cord which can be bought from most electrical or hardware shops. So virtually any room, from garden shed to attic, can become a photographic laboratory. But the most conveniently converted rooms are the bathroom or the kitchen.

Choosing the room

When selecting a room it is helpful to consider these points.
● Can the room be screened easily to shut out light?
● Does the room have a surface long enough to place at least two, and preferably three, dishes side by side? The space needed depends on the size of your developing dishes. As a guide, 12 x 15in (30 x 37cm) dishes need a length of about 4ft (120cm). You must also allow space—not on the same work surface, if possible—for the enlarger.
● Can the room be made, and kept, clean? Dust and dirt mar the results in both developing and printing.
● Can electricity be supplied safely?
● Is there enough ventilation? Very small, poorly ventilated rooms are oppressive for any length of time.

A light-tight room

Windows are usually the chief difficulty and a blackout screen is the best solution. It can be made from hardboard, three-ply wood or stiff card fixed to a secure wooden frame. Glue and tack the material to the frame to prevent light leaking in round the edges and paint the screen black on the window-facing surface. Small clips fixed permanently to the window frame will enable you to secure the screen quickly. Minor light leaks can be stopped with 2in (5cm) wide strips of black adhesive tape, or weather stripping

(draught excluder)—which should be painted black if possible—or strips of black foam rubber.

Alternatively, you may find that you can make a blackout screen out of heavy-duty black PVC sheeting, but it may be difficult to seal the edges effectively. A surprising amount of light seeps around door frames (and even through keyholes), so use 2in (5cm) wide black tape, or draught excluder or a heavy, lightproof curtain.

Other possible sources of light leaks include ventilation points and entry points for pipes. Use a venting hood to make ventilators light-tight, so you don't cut off the ventilation. This is *very* important when working in rooms with gas appliances.

Checking for light-tightness: remain patiently inside for at least 10 minutes until your eyes are used to the dark, to check it really is blacked out. Always check the room each time because light can seep into a seemingly black room. It is also important to have the area behind the enlarger black in case leakages of light from the lamphouse reflect off a white wall on to the paper.

The work area

The workbench itself should be covered with washable material (always wipe up any spilled chemicals immediately). Ideally, the enlarger should sit on a separate work surface which is sturdy enough to prevent shake during printing, away from the chemicals in the processing trays to prevent contamination of the paper and to keep electrical equipment away from water. Always be careful about using electricity near water. Have your enlarger grounded (earthed) if this is what the makers advise and *never* touch any switches or plugs with wet or even damp hands. Cord-pull switches are the safest to use.

When using the bathroom as an improvised darkroom you can wash the prints in the bath and a temporary workbench can be conveniently positioned on the bath itself. To raise the surface to a comfortable working height, build the bench on six 12in (30cm) high legs which can be screwed into three pieces of wood 2 x 2in (50 x 50mm), which sit across the bath to support the bench. It does not need to be the full length of the bath as long as there is enough room to work.

Finally, make sure that the door closes firmly and hang a sign outside on the door handle, to prevent anyone bursting in at the wrong moment.

DARKROOM EQUIPMENT
Items marked with an asterisk are useful but not essential.
1 enlarger
2 masking frame* (enlarging easel)
3 printing tongs
4 developing dishes (trays)
5 measuring cylinders (graduates)
6 thermometer
7 fluffless towel
8 waste bin
9 safelight
10 timer with large dial
11 puffer brush*
12 focus finder
13 footswitch for enlarger* or exposure time switch*
14 blackout screen
15 ventilator hood
16 work bench
siphon for washing*, dish warmer* enlarging meter*, RC and flatbed print drier*, (glazer)*, print squeegee*

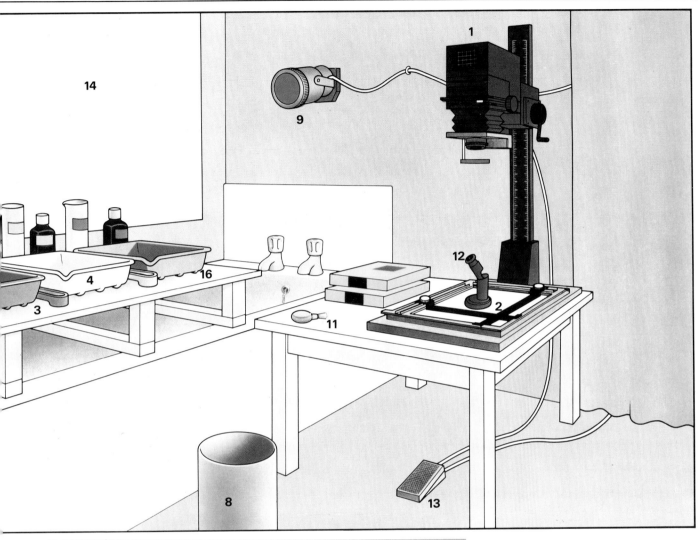

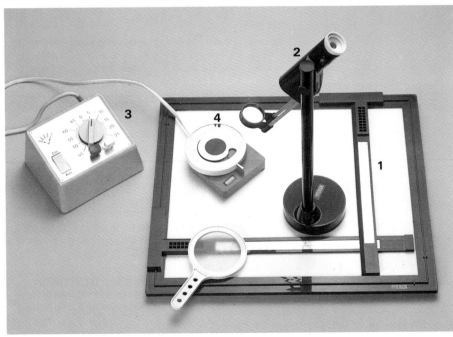

1 A masking frame holds the paper flat on the baseboard. It is more economical to buy one that takes a fairly large print—10 x 12in (24 x 30cm). But check that the baseboard is big enough to hold a large enlarging easel, or the easel may not sit evenly on the baseboard.

2 A focus finder is useful to check that the projected image is pin-sharp. Most models let you examine the grain structure of the negative to find the exact focus.

3 An exposure time switch is pre-set. Once switched on it leaves your hands free for techniques such as burning-in or for processing. They can be simple, requiring setting for each exposure or electronic, offering repeats of the same exposure.

4 An enlarger exposure meter works out the correct exposure and saves making test strips.

Creating a permanent darkroom

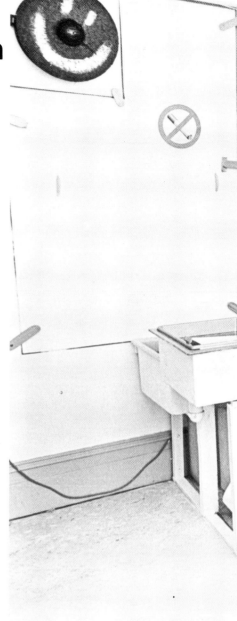

It is the dream of every photographer doing processing at home to own a permanent darkroom. Often this is impossible because of space restrictions within the home, but, if a free area can be found so that you can leave everything set up, you can get down to work straight away at any time. This means faster results.

Choosing a room

The choice is restricted in most households but you are looking for a room which can be blacked out, kept at a reasonable temperature, and to which you can run electricity and water. Basements and lofts can usually be adapted, although lofts tend to become over-hot in summer and cold in the winter. Sheds and outbuildings suffer the same disadvantages but can still be used. Of course, any spare room indoors can be perfect.

Bear in mind that you will be cramped if the room is small. Anything narrower than 6ft (2m) will prevent you from fitting benches down both sides. The length of the room is less important and 6ft (2m) or more will be adequate. On the other hand an enormous room is tiresome as it involves too much walking about—7 x 8ft (2 x 2.5m) is a comfortable size for a small amateur darkroom, while a room 8 x 10ft (2.5 x 3m) is luxurious.

Excluding the light

The first job is to stop the light coming in. Windows can be covered with hardboard or chipboard, either nailed in place or, better still, held by turn-catches so that the board may be removed if necessary. Cut the board to fit on to the main window frame. If light creeps round the edges you can stick a strip of sponge draught excluder, as used for windows, behind the edge of the board to cut it out. An alternative is to use opaque polythene sheeting, fixed in place with strong masking tape all the way round.

The door has to be checked too. If light leaks round the edge fit draught excluder here as well.

Now stand in the room with the lights off for 10 minutes or until your eyes get accustomed to the dark and if you see any chinks of light cut them out with tape, polythene sheeting or other suitable material.

Ventilation

Blocking up all the holes has probably also prevented the entry of fresh air so it is advisable now to arrange for some ventilation, perhaps through the window or door. The ideal is a powered ventilator fan, suitably light-trapped of course, so that air can be extracted efficiently. Do not have a fan blowing into the room as this blows dust about,

▼ The most effective way of excluding light from a permanent darkroom is to cut a piece of chipboard exactly to fit the window frame, using turn-catches so that it can be removed easily.

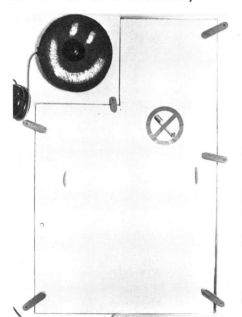

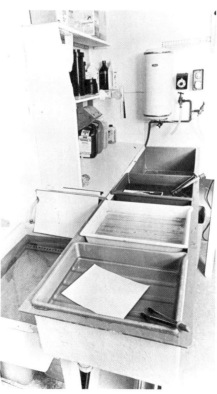

▲ The ideal layout for your darkroom is one which allows you to work efficiently without being constantly on the move. Here the equipment has been carefully arranged. Everything is easily accessible from a central point. The work flows from right to left. All the controls are grouped round the enlarger, the majority being wall-mounted to avoid causing baseboard vibration while printing.

◀ A large fibreglass sink is easier to keep clean than a bench top when processing prints. It also doubles as a water bath to stabilize the temperature of the processing solutions.

▶ A drying rack is easy to make. This one is a series of rectangular frames with a light muslin stretched over each. Ample space between the frames ensures good air circulation.

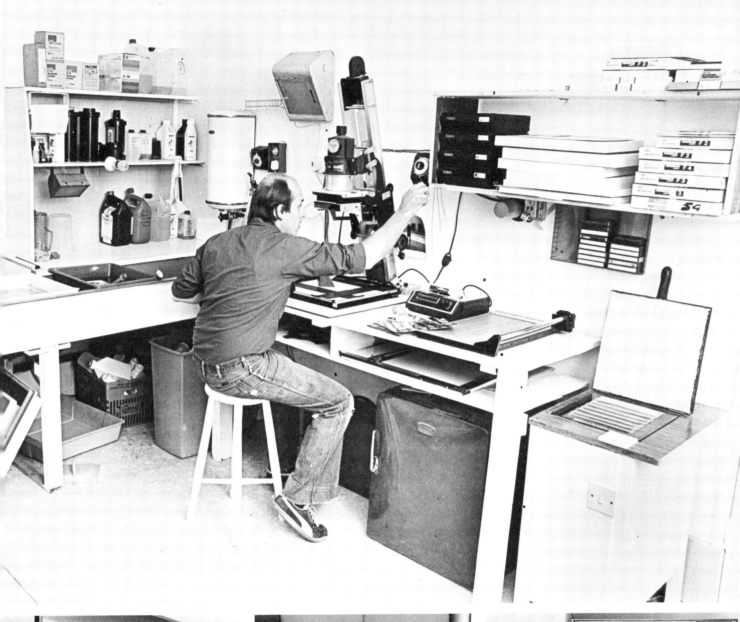

▲ A simple cabinet for making contact sheets. A safelight inside allows the paper and negatives to be positioned. A white light inside is turned on when the lid is down to make the exposure.

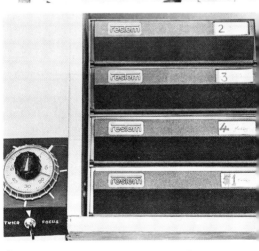

▲ Paper safes are more convenient containers than the original packaging when printing. Keeping them on a shelf within easy reach leaves the working bench free for larger items.

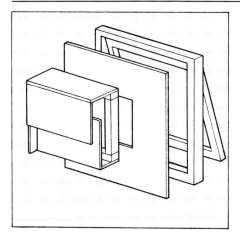

▲ Although a darkroom is light-tight it shouldn't be air-tight. This simply constructed air inlet can be set into the door to give adequate ventilation. An exhaust fan set into a far wall causes the air to circulate.

▶ A division between wet and dry areas is essential, although few people have the space to create such a clear separation as in this ideal layout.

which inevitably lands on films and the enlarger. A simple inlet somewhere else in the room can let air in. Ready-made exhaust (extractor) units are commercially available.

A less expensive answer is a box-shaped channel or double louvres painted matt black inside, set into the window, so that air can enter but light cannot. A small darkroom without any form of ventilation becomes uncomfortable quite quickly.

The main requirements

Now consider the basic layout of the room. The possible combinations of bench and sink arrangement are limitless but bear in mind two basic principles. Firstly, dry work such as enlarging, filing, retouching and mounting must be kept away from wet work such as film processing, print developing and washing. If space prevents two separate benches build a partition 20in (50cm) high to prevent splashes reaching the dry side. Secondly, try to arrange a logical flow of work in one direction, to avoid crossing the room unnecessarily. For example, when making black and white prints you will probably take the negative out of the file, operate the enlarger, develop, stop, fix, wash and dry the print. Organizing the room in that order will save a good deal of time when working.

If your conversion to a darkroom

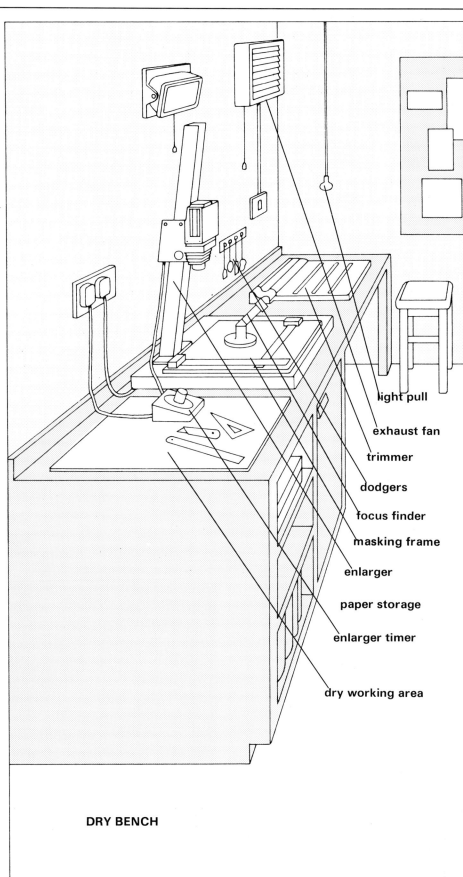

light pull

exhaust fan

trimmer

dodgers

focus finder

masking frame

enlarger

paper storage

enlarger timer

dry working area

DRY BENCH

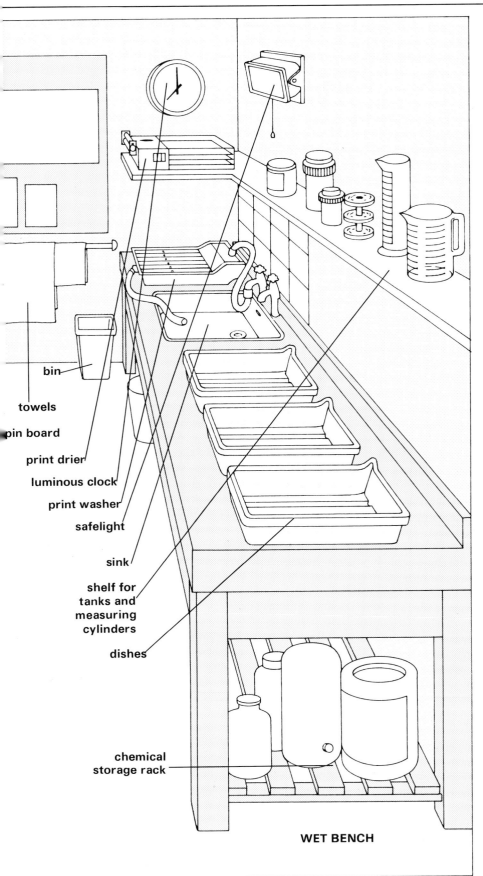

bin

towels

pin board

print drier

luminous clock

print washer

safelight

sink

shelf for
tanks and
measuring
cylinders

dishes

chemical
storage rack

WET BENCH

involves major reconstruction work, such as moving walls, you may need building regulation approval, but if in doubt ask your local authority.

Flooring

Despite the greatest care you will splash water and drip chemicals on to the floor, which must therefore be waterproof. Concrete floors are ideal if properly sealed. Waterproof flooring compounds are available from builders' merchants and are simply painted on. Wood floors are best covered with a complete sheet of flooring material since individual tiles invariably let moisture through the cracks. Choose a flooring which is not slippery when wet. Most kitchen vinyl or linoleum floorings are satisfactory but carpeting is a bad choice because it soaks up water and chemicals. On no account should you have loose mats or rugs in the darkroom as you will almost certainly trip over them.

Walls and ceilings

Despite being called a darkroom it is dreary and uncomfortable to work in dark surroundings. Paint the walls and ceilings with washable paint or emulsion in light colours. White tends to be over-bright on walls but any pale, neutral colour, such as beige, will reflect light from the safelight and improve visibility.

The only place where black paint should be used is on the wall or ceiling near the enlarger since any stray light spilling from the enlarger will not then reflect back on to the printing paper.

Benches and sinks

Dry or wet benches should be at least 20in (50cm) from front to back and preferably 30in (75cm) in order to support an enlarger baseboard. The height of the bench top from the floor would normally be 3ft (1m) or a little more. Measure a few surfaces around the house to find a suitable height, as it is bad for the back as well as uncomfortable to stand bent over all the time. Should you wish to sit while working use a high stool.

Kitchen units are usually fine for a darkroom as long as they are firmly fixed and do not wobble. To make your own bench use 2 x 2in (50 x 50mm) or 1 x 2in (25 x 50mm) wood for the legs and either fit cross-bracing or panel the sides to stop the frame twisting. It is always better to screw the structure firmly to the wall since it is vital that the enlarger does not move or vibrate while printing. Fit the front of the dry bench with hinged or sliding doors. Provide a small under-cut at floor level to tuck your toes under as this lets you stand upright and closer to the bench.

The length of dry bench needed depends on your scale of operations. As well as the width of your enlarger you need somewhere to rest a negative file, perhaps a timer and the packet of printing paper. Never under-estimate the length—6ft (2m) is a reasonable minimum. The length of the wet bench depends on similar principles. Suppose you intend to make black and white prints up to 16 x 20in (40 x 50cm), you will use three trays, taking up more than 4ft (1.2m) on their own, plus washing facilities.

Cover the tops of the benches with a smooth, waterproof surface such as Formica, which is easy to keep clean. At the back of the wet bench fit a 'splash-back', a small strip running the whole length of the bench to prevent liquids dribbling over the back. For the water supply a small domestic sink is quite adequate, especially stainless steel which is chemical resistant. An enamel sink is fine as long as it is not too chipped or the chemicals will corrode the metal base. An excellent alternative is to fit a sink sufficiently large for all the wet work to be done in the sink itself. You will need to support the sink on a sheet of blockboard about ¾in (20mm) thick or it will flex and crack. Such an arrangement is, however, chemical resistant and easy to keep clean.

Installing water

A permanent darkroom without running water is a feasible proposition but having to take wet prints or films elsewhere for washing is inconvenient. A supply of cold water is more important than hot. One hot tap and two cold is ideal because you can wash film or prints whilst making up other solutions, and so on. A mixer tap may seem a good idea, allowing you to wash films in warm water, but has the danger that when a cold tap is turned on elsewhere in the house it reduces the cold water pressure and the film could be damaged by the sudden rise in water temperature.

The sink waste must be suitably trapped and should run into the foul water drainage, like the bath for example, not into rainwater or surface water drains. Be sure to install the sink so that water runs down the plug-hole. Near the sink you will need a towel.

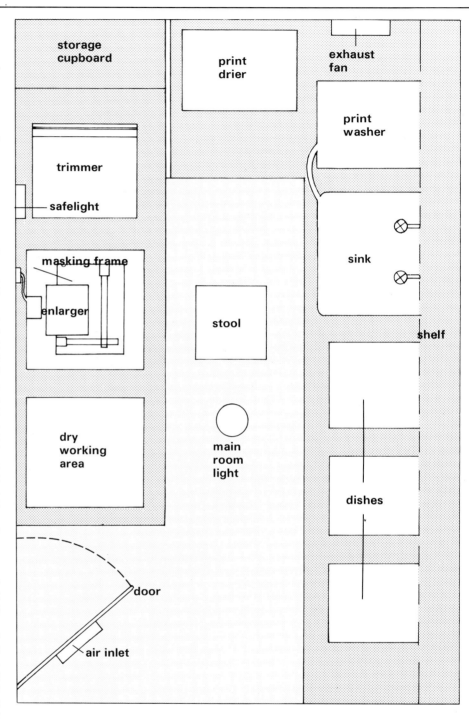

▲ As most people have to make do with a small darkroom, careful planning is essential if the space is to be used to the best advantage.

Smooth linen is preferable to normal terry towels which spread dust and loose fibres.

Illumination

For black-and-white printing you need a safelight, and in a room larger than 6 x 8ft (2 x 2.5m) you may need two. Position a safelight so that it shines well on to the wet bench, making sure it is not closer than the distance recommended by the manufacturer. You will then be able to see clearly what you are doing. Printing papers become much less sensitive to light as soon as they get into the developer so you are unlikely to fog the paper, although you should test it.

It is worth fixing an additional white

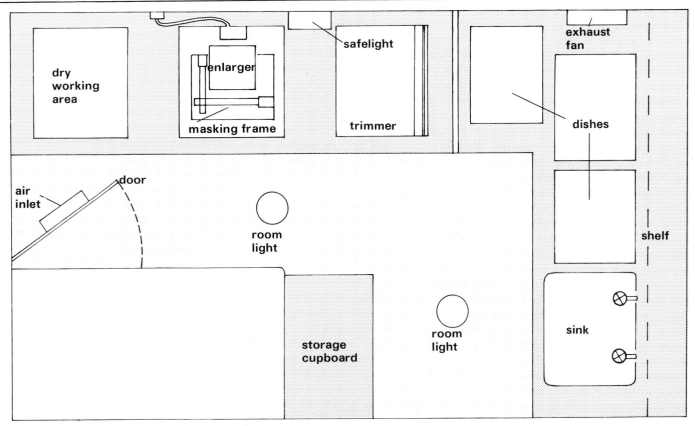

In the diagram:
- dry working area
- enlarger
- masking frame
- safelight
- trimmer
- exhaust fan
- dishes
- shelf
- air inlet
- door
- room light
- room light
- storage cupboard
- sink

▲ Some rooms are more difficult to adapt than others. For instance, it isn't always possible to separate the wet and dry areas. The solution is to fit a partition at least 20in (50cm) high that prevents splashes reaching the dry area. However the work flow should still move in one direction.

light near the print washing area so that you can study test strips and final prints in a good light. If so it should have a ceiling pull-switch. Never place an ordinary light switch, or indeed any switch, where you might be tempted to operate it with wet hands.

Other electrics

You will need mains power for a number of electrical items: enlarger, film or print drier, print exposure meter and so on. The sockets must be grounded (earthed) and wall-mounted above the bench to avoid fiddling at floor level. Keep them all on the dry side of the room, well away from water. A good number, four or more, of well-placed sockets is a boon. Never be tempted to run an extension cord under the door and then use adapters to plug everything into one socket. It is dangerous. If in any doubt about the electrics ask an electrician.

Heating

Try to maintain the room temperature at a steady and comfortable level, perhaps 59−68°F (15−20°C). Radiators from central heating are perfect. Oil-filled electric radiators are fine, as are other electric heaters which do not give out light or much infra-red. Keep them away from the wet side of the room and cover any lights on them. A thermostat light coming on suddenly while you load a film improves visibility but spoils film. Fan heaters are a nuisance because they spread dust. Oil heaters should not be used because the fumes cannot escape easily from a room with less than perfect ventilation. Also avoid heaters which give out light.

Putting things away

It is difficult to provide too much storage space. Cupboards under the dry bench will store paper, negative files and the bigger pieces of equipment, while drawers are useful for small items. Under the wet bench you will be keeping trays, tanks and other large wet items so it is probably better to leave open shelves or racks—definitely not drawers, which will trap damp. The best place for measures, small tanks, bottles of chemicals, the clock and so on, is on a shelf above the wet bench or sink.

A 10in (25cm) shelf with a small lip at the front edge to stop things falling off is about right. Further shelves higher up will store the items used less often. If you put up a shelf above the dry bench do not position it in the way of the enlarger.

Cleaning up

After each session you must throw away the exhausted chemicals and pour into storage containers those solutions you wish to keep. Wash out all the wet equipment carefully and put it away tidily so that next time it is clean and ready to use. Unwashed utensils leave chemical deposits which will contaminate subsequent processes and spoil your results. Dishes of solution left out days will evaporate, making the solution unusable and the damp will corrode metal equipment. You should occasionally go round the room with a vacuum cleaner to remove dust. For the waste material you produce during printing sessions, the used test strips and the reject prints, a waste-bin will be needed. Get a plastic one. Metal ones rust and wicker ones let water drip through onto the floor.

Once you have done all this you can move all your gear in, spread it out and get to work.

Darkroom accessories: the dry bench

1 All dry bench work is
centred on the enlarger.
2 The Paterson Micro
Focus finder is designed
for low magnification printing.
3 An adjustable masking
frame allows the width of
the print border to be
varied.
4 The Paterson Enlarging
Meter overcomes the need
for test strips each time a
print is made.
5 The Saunders Borderless
Easel uses sliding metal
arms to retain the paper.
6 The Paterson Major
Focus Finder is used for
high magnification work.
7 An accurate timer
ensures that exposures are
consistent from print
to print.
8 Clear markings on a
rotary trimmer and a self-
sharpening blade make
print trimming easy.
9 This large safelight gives
a directional light that can
be angled to suit the
printer.

Such a large amount of darkroom
equipment is available these days that it
is difficult for the amateur to decide
what will be useful and effective. It is
easy to be persuaded by advertisements
or salesmen that an expensive item is
necessary when its uses are, in fact,
limited. Even basic items such as trays
or thermometers vary a great deal in
quality and design so that a little basic
information can be a great help.

Safelights

The first essential for a safelight is that
there should be no danger of it fogging
your printing paper. The second is that
it should let you see what you are doing.
Professionals often have a large safelight suspended from the ceiling above
their head to give an even lighting to
the darkroom, smaller ones being
positioned to throw a brighter light over
the processing area. The amateur rarely
has the space or money for this. One

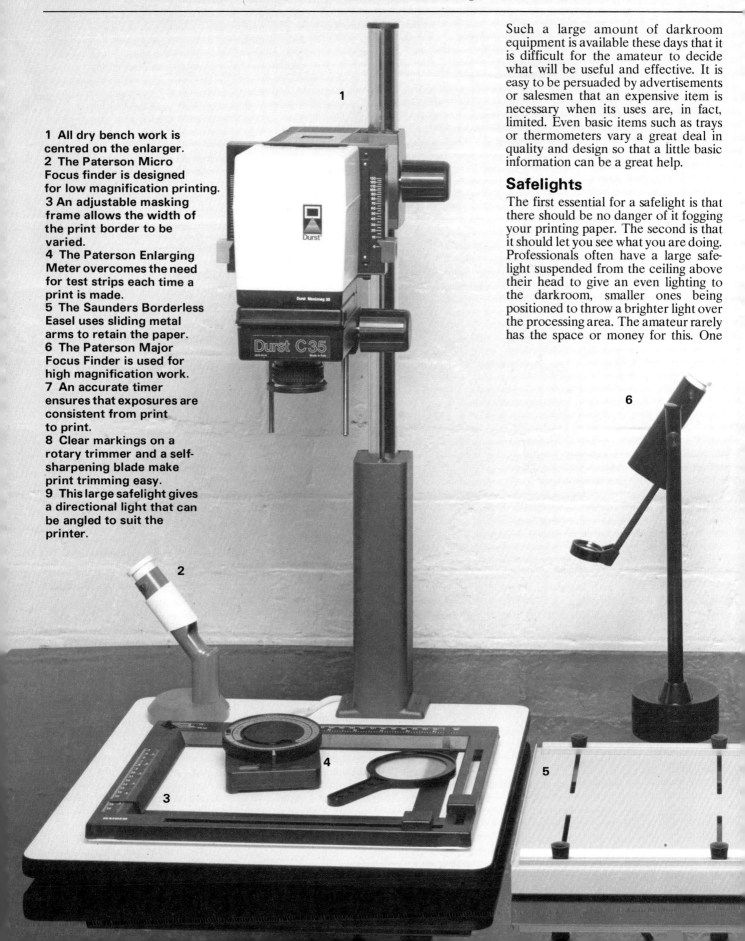

safelight or at the most two should satisfy his needs.

Though they are not cheap the safelights, such as those made by Kodak, in the form of metal or plastic lamphouses which use flat filters are the best available. They give a fairly directional light and can be positioned so that they do not shine into your eyes. Safelights made in the form of plastic domes give good general illumination but should not come into your field of view since they can dazzle you while printing.

It is a mistake to use a dark green safelight when loading reels with film. Modern materials are very sensitive and will be fogged by even a brief exposure to any form of safelight. Very dark amber or olive green safelights are available for colour printing, but if they give enough light to let you see the darkroom equipment they are almost certainly unsafe.

Provided you follow the manufacturer's instructions you should have no trouble with fogging. Secondhand safelights are a different matter: the filter can easily fade with prolonged use and produce fogging.

If in the slightest doubt, expose a small sheet of paper under the enlarger, giving an exposure that will result in a medium to light grey tone after development. Place the exposed paper emulsion side up at the normal working distance from the safelight, at the same time covering a quarter of it with a piece of card. After one minute cover half the paper, and after another minute three-quarters of it. Leave the final quarter for two more minutes. Now process the sheet.

The first three steps should all be the same density, though the one that had four minutes will probably have a darker tone of grey. If there is a difference in density between the first three steps the safelight is either too close, is fitted with too powerful a bulb or the filter has faded.

Masking frames

These are also known as 'enlarging easels' or 'printing frames'. There are two basic designs. One produces prints with a white border, the paper being held flat by metal arms that form a frame covering the edges of the paper. Many models have devices for adjusting the width of the margin to suit your particular preference.

The other type of frame produces prints without borders. On some models the corners of the paper are held by friction, using small right-angled metal grips. On others the surface of the frame is permanently sticky. The sticky surface is especially suitable for those RC papers that curl with the emulsion bowed outwards, since such papers are particularly difficult to hold flat with corner grips. Unfortunately the surface gradually loses its stickiness and must be renewed from time to time by spraying with an aerosol adhesive.

When deciding on the size of frame to purchase it is a mistake to buy a very large one for general use as it will prove awkward to handle when making smaller sized prints. An 11 x 14in (25 x 30cm) easel is ideal for making prints up to 8 x 10in (25.4 x 20.3cm). Make sure that the one you buy has a non-slip base, perhaps covered with foam plastic. If it has not, the easel may move slightly as the paper is inserted.

9

7

8

Focusing magnifiers

Some focusing magnifiers use a comparatively low magnification, showing enlarged details of the image. There is no need to bring the eye close to the lens with this type as the image can be viewed from a variety of angles.

Aerial magnifiers greatly enlarge the image of the grain of the negative which snaps in and out of focus and allows the focusing mechanism of the enlarger to be adjusted with great precision. However, to work well the instrument must be placed in the centre of the image on the baseboard and the eye must be close to the magnifying lens. It is difficult to do this when making a big print since you have to stretch up a long way to reach the enlarger's focusing knob. To overcome these difficulties Paterson make two versions, the 'Micro' for normal degrees of enlargement and the 'Major' for big ones. The low-powered focusing magnifiers are rapid and easy to use under any conditions, the more powerful ones are probably more precise.

Print trimmers

The old type of guillotine trimmer, where the paper or card was cut by pulling down a large curved blade, is not readily available today and, unless used with an efficient guard, unsafe. Its advantage was that it could cut very heavy board effectively.

Modern trimmers, such as the one shown here, are usually of the rotary type. The print is positioned on the baseboard and a rotating wheel with a very sharp edge in a protective holder is pulled along a guide bar, cutting through the paper as it moves. The circular blade is self-sharpening and cuts even very thin paper cleanly and accurately, but there is a limit to the thickness of board that can be cut—usually about $\frac{1}{16}$ in (1.5mm).

To retain its sharpness the blade must be in contact with the guiding edge all the time. It is, therefore, important that the guide rail, which supports the blade as it moves along, is rigid. If the baseboard is made from plywood it should be thick enough to prevent warping, while if it is metal it must not bend under pressure.

The scale against which the top edge of the print rests should be marked in both inches and millimetres. It is helpful if it also carries indications of the standard print sizes. It is essential that the scale remains at right angles to the guiding edge. If in any doubt about this, check it with a set square.

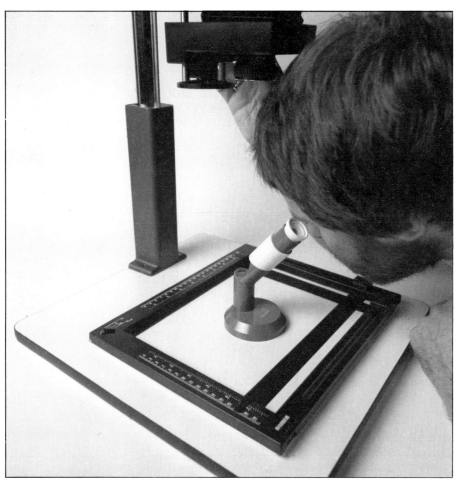

◀ The most accurate way of focusing is to use a grain magnifier such as the Paterson Micro Focus Finder.

◀ Below: a well made print trimmer with a firm guide bar to support the blade holder is safer and more practical than a craft knife and a ruler.

▶ Although this type of timer is expensive, the initial outlay is more than justified by the consistency gained, which helps to avoid the waste of cruder timing methods.

▼ Once it has been set up, an enlarging meter, such as the Paterson, saves time and paper.

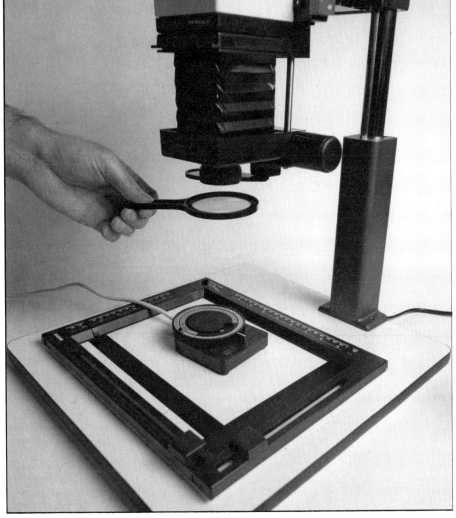

Timers

An inexpensive clockwork-operated timer is suitable for timing the processing of films and paper, provided the dial is large enough and clear enough to be read under safelight conditions. There is no point in buying a luminous type unless you are processing colour or panchromatic material in an open tray. The plastic timers designed for the kitchen are rarely clear or accurate enough for photographic use.

When exposing the paper, an electric timer that can be preset to switch the enlarger on and off, is to be preferred. The most useful sort are those which it is possible to set to exposures as short as one second or as long as 90 or 100 seconds. For greater accuracy the scale is often spread over two dials, one reading from one to 10 and the other from 10 to 100. The exposure is started by pressing a button. Unfortunately, some of the older types need so much pressure that vibration can be transmitted to the enlarger column. Such timers should be avoided. The lighter the touch needed the better.

The accuracy of electric timers can be affected by long periods in a humid darkroom. Instead of wiring one permanently to the enlarger, plugs should be used so that it can be stored in a dry atmosphere after use.

Enlarging exposure meters

These can be divided into two basic types, both of which can be used for black-and-white and colour. With the first you set the enlarging lens to the stop you prefer and the meter gives the length of exposure needed. With the second the exposure time is set and the meter indicates the aperture needed.

The advantage claimed for the latter is that, when making colour prints, very short or very long exposures cause a shift in colour balance. However, since the aperture of the lens will vary widely with this type of meter it is best used with top quality lenses that will give sharp results with all apertures.

The justification for 'variable time' meters is that all enlarging lenses have one aperture that gives the best result and this is the one that should be used, the exposure being varied to suit.

Both types can give accurate results once you have learnt how to use them and know how to judge the most suitable section of the image to use for the reading. Both are rapid in operation, but remember that an ordinary test strip will probably be as accurate and will give you more information.

Choosing an enlarger

Undoubtedly, the most important piece of darkroom equipment is the enlarger, which is a special type of projector (similar in principle to a slide projector). With it, you can make an enlargement of the whole negative or select a portion of it and print just that area, which makes the enlarger a very creative photographic tool.

A new enlarger will probably be the most expensive item in your darkroom. Knowing how an enlarger works, and what designs are available will help you decide which model is best suited to your needs.

All photographic enlargers do basically the same thing. They project an image on to a sheet of sensitive material to make a print. Every enlarger has a light source, a means of directing the light, a carrier to hold the negative and a lens to focus the illuminated image. These components are integrated into one unit known as the 'enlarger head', which is supported on a rigid column. This is attached to a baseboard, which also acts as a surface on which to place the printing paper or a printing easel. Some models can be wall-mounted for extra stability.

In normal use, the negative carrier, the lens and the baseboard should be kept parallel, although the distances between them can be altered to change the size of the projected image and to focus it.

The main differences among enlargers lie in the light source and whether they are designed primarily for black-and-white or for colour work.

Colour enlargers are similar to those for black-and-white, except that they need facilities for introducing colour filters somewhere between the light source and the negative. This may be a drawer for gelatin filters or a special colour head which incorporates the filters into a mechanism connected to a set of colour coded dials.

Types of enlarger

It is most important that any light source provides even illumination over the whole of the negative area and there are three ways to achieve this. There is the condenser system, the diffuser system, or a happy combination of both, known as a condenser-diffuser or semi-diffused system. Both condenser and condenser-diffuser types are usually only suitable for printing negatives up to 5 x 4in (12.7 x 10.2cm).

Condenser-diffuser enlargers: most amateurs and many professionals use enlargers which have this mixed system.

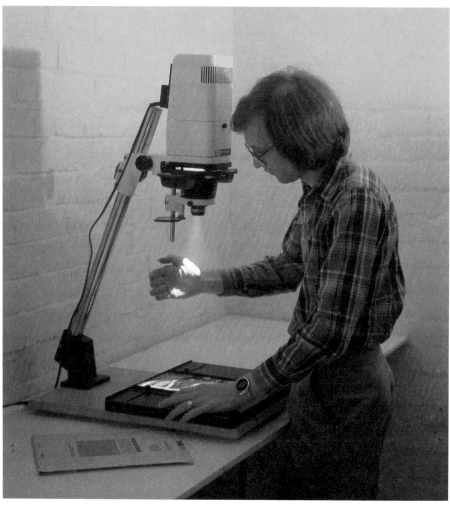

It includes an opal light-bulb to diffuse the light and a pair of condensers (or sometimes just one) to focus the light, after it has passed through the negative, as a brief patch of light on the enlarging lens.

Direct light condenser enlargers: use a point source lamp (bulb) and the condensers focus the light on to the lens as a bright point of light. One of their characteristics is that they give a rather contrasty image, owing to the Callier effect. With this effect, light passing through the negative is partially absorbed and scattered by the silver grains in the emulsion, while in the clear areas light passes through freely.

Diffuser enlargers: since negatives larger than 5 x 4in (12.7 x 10.2cm) need big condensers for even illumination, diffusion lighting is used, especially in professional darkrooms, for enlarging negatives 5 x 4in (12.7 x 10.2cm) and upwards. The light usually comes from a type of fluorescent tube called a cold cathode source behind a diffusing screen

▲ **The enlarger is vital equipment in the making of a print, and should be chosen carefully. Check whether the price includes a lens, as not all enlargers are supplied with one.**

and, unlike the condenser enlarger, it stays cool all the time.

Most colour enlargers, for any size of negative, use a diffused light system and usually have a halogen lamp.

Lenses

To do justice to a negative you need a first-class enlarging lens. Wide aperture lenses cost more but give a brighter image for easier focusing.

Standard focal length lenses for the most popular negative formats are:

110 — 30mm	6 x 6cm — 80mm
35mm — 50mm	6 x 7cm — 90mm

The magnification you can achieve with any enlarger depends not only on the film-to-baseboard distance, but also on the focal length of the lens in use.

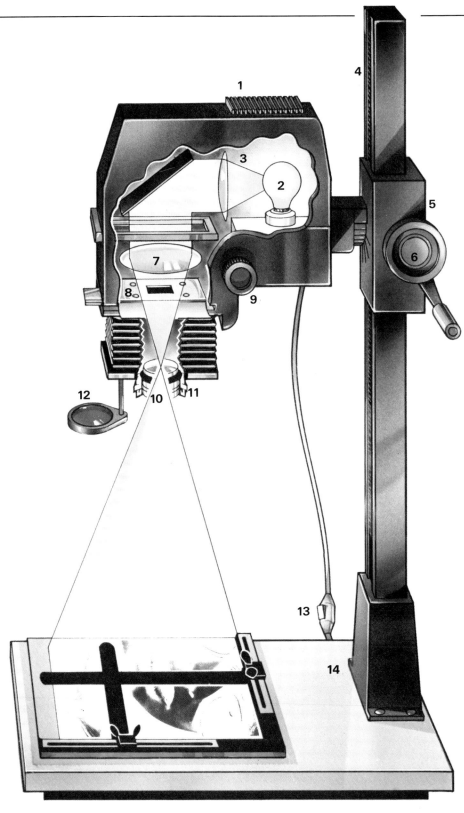

A condenser-diffuser enlarger

1 VENTILATION FOR LAMPHOUSE

2 BULB This must be an enlarger bulb of the correct wattage for that size of lamphouse. The manufacturer or your dealer will advise you if in doubt. An adjuster mechanism focuses the bulb for different negative sizes or very large enlargements.

3 LAMPHOUSE

4 ENLARGER COLUMN Enlargers with heavy heads may have twin or flat columns for additional rigidity.

5 HEAD LINKAGE TO COLUMN Many linkages have a locking wheel for rotating the head through 90° to project on to a wall for giant enlargements.

6 HEAD TRANSPORT This device may simply free the head so that it can be raised (to make the image on the paper bigger) or lowered (to make it smaller), or it may move the head by friction or by rack and pinion drive.

7 CONDENSERS Condensers focus the light sharply on to the negative and must be large enough to cover the whole negative area.

8 NEGATIVE CARRIER

9 LENS FOCUSING WHEEL This device works the lens focusing system which may be bellows or telescopic tubes, altering the distance between the lens and the negative to produce a sharply projected image.

10 LENS Some enlargers take different focal length lenses for use with different negative sizes but a lens which prints 35mm negatives will also print 126, 110, and portions of larger negatives.

11 f STOPS As on a camera, these stops control the amount of light by varying the aperture of the lens. Click stops are helpful as you can feel each change of f stop.

12 RED FILTER In black-and-white printing this filter is swung in front of the lens to prevent the paper being exposed while it is being positioned under the enlarger.

13 SWITCH for light in lamphouse.

14 BASEBOARD

Darkroom accessories: the wet bench

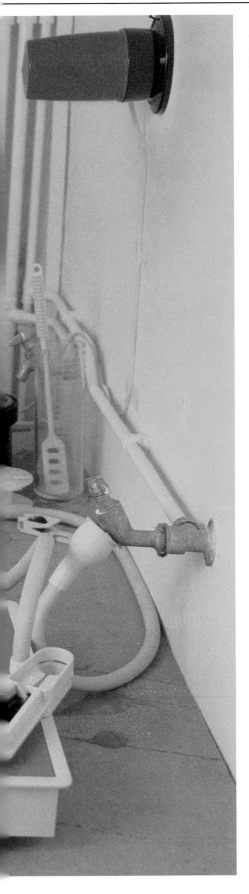

Equipment used in the wet area of the darkroom tends to be subject to quite a lot of wear and tear. The quality of equipment is therefore important, and knowledge of the limitations of each item helps in making wise purchases.

Dishes (trays)

The most practical material is undoubtedly plastic, though it should be of a fairly thick gauge so that it will stand up to hard use and not twist or bend when the dish is rocked. Stainless steel may last a lifetime but is far too expensive for the average amateur, while enamelled steel tends to chip and crack.

Many photographers prefer to use dishes one size larger than the print they are making. This ensures that there is plenty of room for the tongs or fingers to grip the print and lift it out of the solution. Sizes smaller than 8 x 10in (20 x 25cm) are inconvenient to use, even when making very small prints. Unless you intend to process small sheets of film, 8 x 10in (20 x 25cm) should be regarded as the minimum size of dish worth buying. To make it easy to identify each solution it is a good idea to use dishes of different colours and always to use the dish for the same solution. Several manufacturers sell their dishes in multi-coloured packs of three with this in mind.

Thermometers

There are three types of photographic thermometers: those with a glass tube filled with mercury or alcohol (a dye being added to the latter to make it visible); those with a metal tube and dial with a pointer on top; and the electronic kind with a digital readout.

Electronic thermometers are very accurate and can be read in the dark, but unfortunately they are expensive. Those with a metal tube and dial are also easy to read but some of the cheaper models are not very accurate. Consequently most amateurs prefer to use the commonly available glass thermometers.

The very cheapest alcohol-filled thermometers can be inaccurate by several degrees, making precision processing

◀ Organize the wet side of the darkroom so each item is where you use it. To avoid chemical contamination place trays in the order used—developer, stop bath, fix, wash—each with its own print tongs. Wash everything well between sessions. Dirt in the jaws of the print squeegee will scratch prints.

impossible If you wish to buy one of these it makes sense to pay a little extra for a reputable one certified to within 0.5°F (0.3°C). If you are doing your own colour processing the greater accuracy of a mercury-filled model, which should be certified to within 0.25°F (0.14°C), is essential. The scales on many photographic thermometers only go up to about 86°F (30°C), so if you are going to process modern colour materials check the thermometer scale reaches at least 104°F (40°C) before you buy it.

Once you have bought a thermometer there is a great temptation to use it as an occasional stirring rod. As glass thermometers are very fragile, such misuse should be avoided.

Print washers

The water in an efficient print washer must change constantly and the prints must be separated. It follows that trying to use a sink or bath is rarely successful.

When you buy a print washer it is essential that it is large enough to take the biggest size of paper that you use regularly or are likely to use in the future. Just because you are making 8 x 10in (20 x 25cm) prints now does not necessarily mean you will not make bigger ones as you gain skill and confidence. However, a washing tank for big prints can take up a lot of valuable space and you will need to balance this against the convenience gained when deciding on the size to buy. One of the characteristics of resin-coated printing paper is that it absorbs little of the processing solutions and, therefore, is easily washed. The Paterson High Speed Print Washer takes advantage of this. The water circulation is particularly effective and prints are thoroughly washed in two to four minutes.

Print driers

There are two types of print driers, those meant for traditional fibre-based papers and those for resin-coated papers; they are not interchangeable.

For amateur use the first type comes in the form of a flat metal box with a slightly curved top surface. The prints are pressed into contact with the heated surface by a tensioned cloth. An electric element inside the box heats the surface evenly. Matt prints are placed on the surface emulsion uppermost. Glossy prints can be dried in the same way or squeegeed emulsion down on to a special chromium-plated sheet available at dealers. This is placed on the

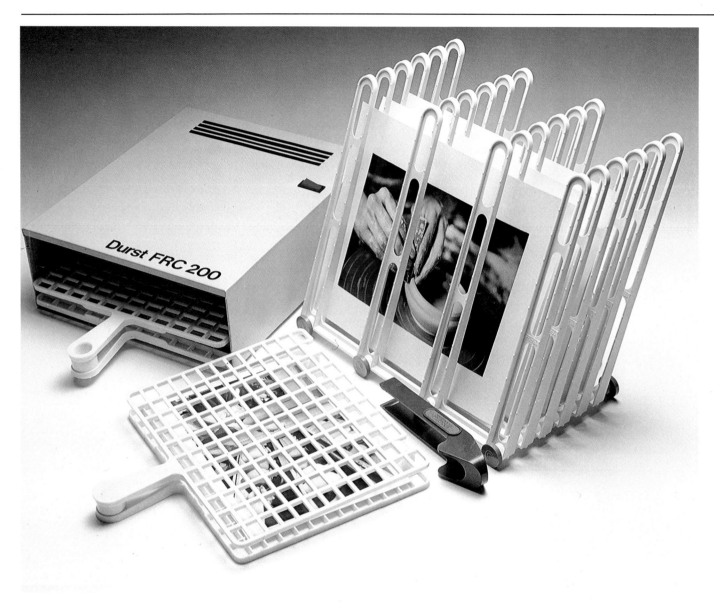

drier, prints uppermost, and the cloth is pulled down over it to keep the prints in contact with the sheet as they dry. The dried prints have a very glossy finish.

If you produce a lot of prints, it might be worth investing in a drier such as the Kaiser 4040, which has two heated surfaces.

Driers for resin-coated paper are designed in a completely different way. Because the paper does not absorb much fluid, it can be dried in a current of warm air instead of on a heated surface. Expensive professional models work on a continuous flow system in which the prints are fed into the machine through powered rollers. They are transported through the machine automatically and emerge dry in a very short time.

Models for the amateur are designed with wire racks on to which the prints are laid while hot air blows over them. Some amateur models do have rollers, but these are hand-operated and merely remove surplus water from the print surface. If you are producing a large number of prints a relatively sophisticated model such as the Durst FRC400 drier which has four print racks and temperature control of the blower will be useful. But such driers are rather expensive and can only be justified if you do a lot of printing over a long period.

Storage containers

Some people try to save money by storing their chemicals in screw-cap soft drink or beer bottles. This is not only dangerous if children are around,

▲ It is possible to dry modern resin-coated printing materials by hanging them on a line and letting them drip dry. However, that takes up a lot of space and is less efficient than the Paterson Print Drying Rack. The Durst FRC 200 Drier, which blows hot air across the print surface, is quicker but is much more expensive.

but, since the metal cap can react with acid solutions, ineffective. Amber glass bottles or opaque plastic containers, with airtight plastic screw caps, are much safer and give better protection from oxidation while the container is full.

As the contents are used the air space above the liquid in the container increases and if developer is being stored oxidation can easily occur. The chance

Processing trays

Chemical mixer

Storage bottles

Thermometer

▲ When choosing accessories it is essential to select those that are robust enough to withstand the wear and tear of darkroom use.

▶ The Paterson High Speed Print Washer provides effective water circulation so that residual chemicals are washed from the print very quickly.

of deterioration can be reduced by using a number of small bottles instead of one large one. Alternatively, a crushable container with folding sides, such as the 'Air Evac' bottle, can be used. Every time some of the liquid is decanted, the top of the container is pressed down until the solution comes level with the neck of the bottle. The cap is then screwed on and air excluded until the developer is used again.

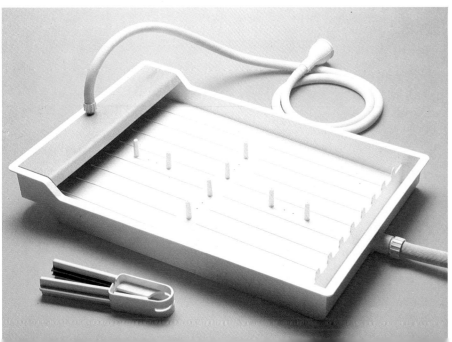

Developing black-and-white film

The camera can only do so much; a good deal of the quality of a fine photograph lies in the developing and printing. By doing your own you have more control over the outcome. You can make the print from just part of the negative, increase or decrease the contrast, lighten or darken parts of the picture to obtain more shadow or highlight detail and choose the paper surface you prefer. But, above all, you have the immense satisfaction of creating the end product yourself.

The basic chemicals and equipment needed to develop black-and-white film are simple and relatively inexpensive and if you cannot afford an enlarger you can always join a camera club which has darkroom equipment. Many amateurs also process colour slide and colour negative film at home and make their own colour prints. But first it is advisable to learn about processing with black-and-white film.

This section shows you how to develop your own black-and-white films; a subsequent one shows how to make contact sheets from them, explaining how to judge the quality of the negatives.

How developing works

When you release the shutter, light enters the camera and falls on the light-sensitive emulsion on the film. The emulsion contains light-sensitive silver halide salts that react according to the brightness of the light they receive. At this stage the changes in the emulsion are invisible and must be 'developed' with chemicals.

The *developer* turns these exposed silver salts into visible black metallic silver—a lot where the light was bright and less where it was dull. The film must remain in the developer for exactly the right length of time. Then the *stop bath* is used. The stop bath simultaneously arrests the action of the developer and neutralizes its alkalinity so that it will not affect the potency of the next chemical, the *fixer*.

At this stage the film carries a black negative image but the rest of the emulsion, which contains unchanged silver salts, remains creamy as before. The fixer removes all the undeveloped silver salts from the emulsion, leaving it transparent in these areas. The film is now in negative form.

Next the film is washed thoroughly to remove all trace of the fixer. If fixer is left on the film, in time it will cause staining. A few drops of *wetting agent* are added to the final wash. This helps to prevent drops of water clinging to the

drying negatives, which may mark them. Most tap water contains fine particles of rust and grit, which can settle on the film and cause white spots on your prints; an inexpensive water filter fitted to your tap will prevent this.

Buying the equipment

Most photographic dealers stock the basic equipment and will advise you on its use. A universal developing tank will accept different film sizes or develop two 35mm films together. Plastic tanks are widely favoured for general use but the more expensive stainless steel ones last longer.

Ideally, your timer should be a pre-set type that rings at the end of a given period. However, you could use a kitchen timer, a watch, or a clock with a second hand.

You will need one 600ml plastic measure for each chemical with a waterproof label. If you find it difficult to judge small quantities, a 45ml plastic measure may be useful.

Preparing the chemicals

Developers and fixers come in either concentrated liquid or powder forms. Powders are less expensive than liquids, but liquids are much easier to handle and are recommended here.

The first step is to read the leaflets carefully as tanks and chemicals come with a bewildering array of instructions. After you have read the various instructions it is an excellent idea to make a preparation chart like the one shown below. But don't just put down the dilution as indicated on the chemical bottle; calculate the actual amount of chemical concentrate plus the amount of water to provide enough solution to cover the film in the developing tank.

Concentrated solutions last for about 6 months, and diluted stop bath and fixer can be kept and re-used. But diluted developer usually has a short life. It is sensible to use a 'one-shot' developer which you throw away after use and so process every film in fresh solution.

Preparation chart
READ THE INSTRUCTIONS AND SET DOWN ON A SHEET OF PAPER:

Dilutions required for chemicals (see instructions with each chemical)	Total amount of liquid needed to cover the film (see tank instructions)
developer	Development time for the type of black and white film you are processing (see developer instructions)
stop bath	
fixer	Time required for fixer (see fixer instructions)

You will need:

EQUIPMENT

1 Universal developing tank
2 Black-and-white film
3 Large jug
4 Mercury thermometer
5 Three 600ml and one 45ml plastic measure
6 Deep plastic basin
7 Timer
8 Plastic or glass funnel
9 Plastic or glass mixing rod
10 Sink with running water
11 Two glass or plastic bottles
12 Photographic hose unit
13 Film clips
14 Drying line (not shown)
15 Film squeegee
16 Scissors
17 Negative storage envelopes

CHEMICALS

18 One-shot developer
19 Stop bath
20 Rapid-type fixer
21 Wetting agent

With diluted fixer and stop bath, it is very important to label bottles with the name of the chemical, the dilution and date of dilution.

Prepare dilutions of chemicals accurately. A dilution might be given as 1 + 9 (one part chemical plus nine parts water). You could use 10ml of chemical and 90ml of water to give 100ml of diluted chemical. If this is not enough, increase each amount, for example, three times to 30ml of chemical and 270ml of water. Always add the chemical first and make up to volume with water. Then stir steadily to mix. After you have prepared one solution be sure to wash everything *very carefully* to prevent contamination when making up the next chemical.

Photographic chemicals often cause dermatitis or trigger allergies so wear rubber or plastic gloves when mixing. Observe a clinical cleanliness at all times, washing away spilt chemicals at once with plenty of water. Always use plastic, glass or stainless steel equip-ment to prepare the chemicals. Never use aluminium, tin, galvanized or copper utensils for mixing or storing them. Finally, store chemicals safely, well away from the reach of children.

Allow enough time

The process of developing a film will take about an hour to complete. Timing is crucial during development, so make sure you will not be interrupted. It would not, however, hurt if you had to leave film in fixer for 10 minutes.

Loading the tank

You load the film on to a reel (also called a spiral) which then sits inside the tank body. This needs practice as you must load the tank 'blind' in total darkness. Any glimmer of light will damage the film, so use a light-tight cupboard, or a room at night with the curtains drawn. Make sure no light comes through cracks round the door. (The setting up of a proper darkroom is described in an earlier section.)

Practise first in the light with an out-dated film (ask your dealer if he has one). Then try loading the reel with your eyes closed to see if you are still adept. Having mastered the knack, you will be ready to process your first film. Remember that unless the reel is absolutely dry the film may stick; many people keep them in drying cabinets. Make sure your hands are absolutely dry too. If your hands start to sweat while you are in the process of loading the reel, lay the reel and film on the clean work bench and dry your hands.

To prepare film for loading

Always prepare an exposed film for loading in *total darkness* and have the parts of the tank laid before you on the work surface.

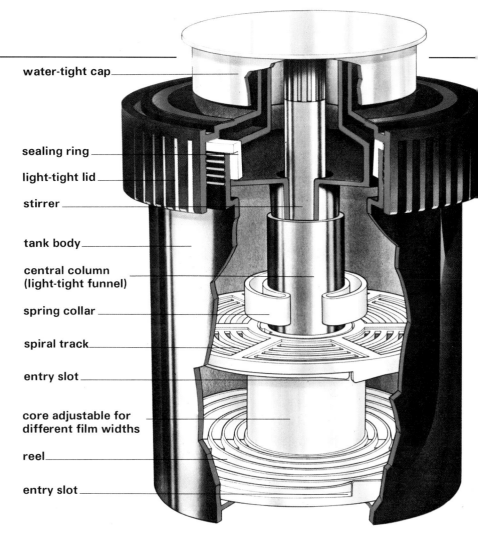

water-tight cap

sealing ring

light-tight lid

stirrer

tank body

central column (light-tight funnel)

spring collar

spiral track

entry slot

core adjustable for different film widths

reel

entry slot

Preparing the film

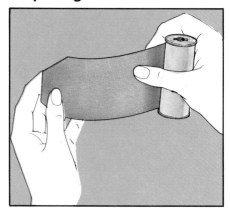

ROLL FILM
Break seal, unwind backing paper until you reach the film; let the film roll up in your hand. When you reach the seal at the end, between the paper and the film, tear it off and let paper and spool drop to the floor.
Straighten out the end of the film, ready for loading into the reel.
A blue background indicates that an operation must be carried out in total darkness. A white background indicates that the light may be switched on.

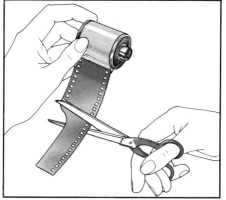

35mm FILM
If the tongue of the film protrudes from the jaws of the cassette, gently pull it out until the full width is reached. Cut it across with scissors between a pair of perforations. *This step can be done with the light switched on.*
In the *dark,* open the cassette by prising off the cap with a bottle opener or special device. If the tongue has been wound inside, open the cassette and cut the film by feel.

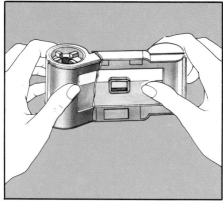

110 and 126 FILM
Break open the cartridge by snapping it into two with your thumbs. Remove the pieces of plastic cartridge from around the film spool and unwind the film to separate it from its backing paper, separating it from the film so the film rolls up in your hand. When you reach the seal at the end, tear off the film and let the spool and paper fall to the floor. Note that most reels are not suitable for 110 film.

Loading a plastic reel

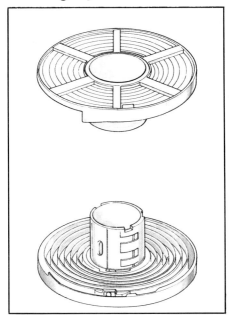

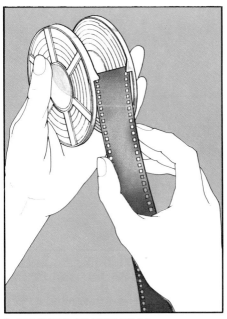

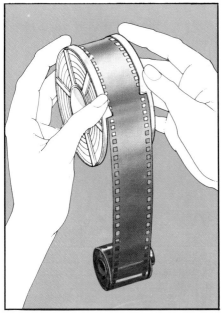

1 ADJUSTING THE REEL
Reels adjust to take different film widths—35mm or 126, 127 and 120 or 220. Some reels are also available which adjust to 110 film. If you need to adjust the reel, follow the instructions carefully. You may jam it permanently if you do the wrong thing.

2 FEEDING IN THE FILM
Before you turn out the light, line up the entry slots on the reel so that they face towards you.
In the dark, slip the end of the film into the slots and gently push it—or pull the end—into the reel until you feel resistance, taking care not to kink the film.

3 WINDING ON THE FILM
Rotate each half of the reel alternately back and forth and the film will feed automatically into the tracks on the reel. If it should jam don't use force; you may tear the film. Remove the film from the reel and start again.

Loading a metal reel

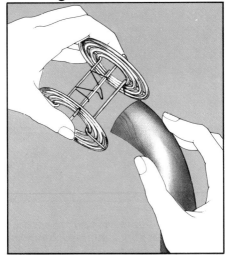

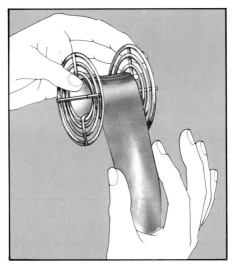

Both types of reel

1 ATTACHING THE FILM
Metal reels do not adjust for different film widths. Hold the reel in one hand with the clip pointing towards the other hand. Push the end of the slightly bowed film between the clip and the spindle. Read the instructions first as designs vary.

2 WINDING ON THE FILM
Hold edges of film with thumb and forefinger so that it is slightly bowed while you rotate the reel away from the film with your other hand. As the edges of the bowed film are released they slot into reel tracks which keep the film surfaces apart.

PLACE REEL IN TANK
Cut or tear the film from its spool and check that the last part is completely wound on to the reel. (The end of a 35mm film will be attached to the spool.) Put the reel into the tank body and screw on the lid.

Step-by-step to developing the negatives

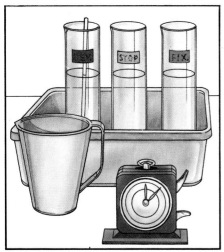

1 PREPARE THE CHEMICALS
Fill the jug with water, adding hot and cold until the temperature is 68°F (20°C). Pour the correct amount of chemical into its measure. Add water from the jug up to the correct volume and stir and mix. Stand the measure in a basin of water at 68°F (20°C). Pre-set timer.

2 POUR IN DEVELOPER
Remove the water-tight cap on the lid. Pour the developer down the light-tight funnel without hesitation (it takes about 10 seconds) and start the timer. Keep the tank upright; never tilt it. Tap the tank, or poke the stirrer down the funnel and swivel the reel to release any air bubbles clinging to the film. Fit the cap.

3 AGITATE THE TANK
Agitate the tank according to the instructions to make sure that fresh developer reaches all parts of the film. You may be instructed to invert the tank, rock it from side to side or twist the stirrer.

6 POUR IN FIXER
Pour in the fixer, replace the cap and start the timer. Agitate for 30 seconds and then every minute.
Fix for the recommended time, but halfway through remove the lid and examine the film. Check that the milkiness has cleared and the film looks virtually black.
Pour fixer into its storage bottle.

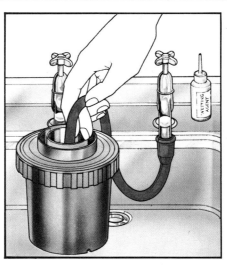

7 WASH THE FILM
Run the cold tap. Check temperature of water. A sudden extreme change of temperature may damage the emulsion. Mix water in the jug to adjust the temperature gradually with several washes if the tap water is too cold. Put the end of the hose in the centre of the reel. Let the water run for 30 minutes. Turn off the tap. Add the recommended amount of wetting agent to the water in the tank. Agitate for 30 seconds. Remove the reel and shake off the water.

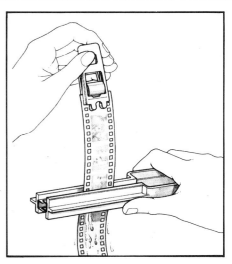

8 WIPE THE FILM
Attach a film clip to the film and gently draw it out of the reel.
Hook the clip over a taut drying line. Wipe away as much water as possible by drawing the film squeegee slowly down the film. (In an emergency you can dip your fingers in water and use them like a squeegee.)
Fix a film clip to the bottom to stop the film curling.
Dry in a dust-free area away from direct heat.

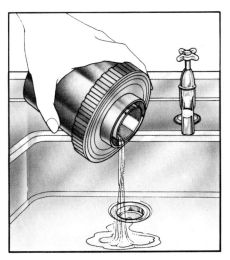

4 REMOVE DEVELOPER
When the timer rings, remove the cap and pour the developer down the sink. (Remember: with one-shot developer you do *not* keep and re-use the diluted chemical.)

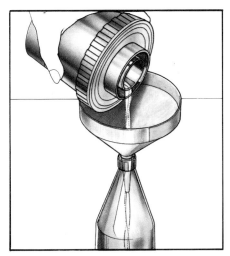

5 USING THE STOP BATH
Quickly pour the stop bath into the tank and refit the cap. Agitate for 15 seconds and then leave for 30 seconds.
Using the washed funnel, pour the stop bath into a bottle labelled with chemical and dilution date. This can be reused until it changes colour.

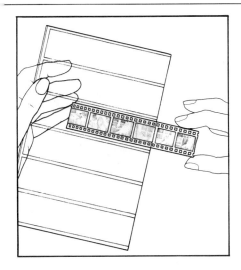

9 STORING NEGATIVES
When completely dry, cut the film into strips: six negatives for 35mm and 126 film; three or four with 120 film. Store each strip in a separate negative storage envelope. Always remember to handle strips only by the edges. Now you have a set of negatives ready for printing.

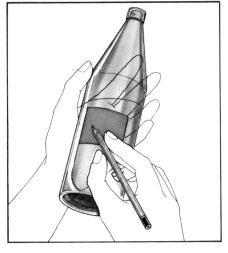

10 KEEP RECORDS
Mark the bottle of fixer with the date and number of films processed. You may like to put vertical marks on the label to represent the number of films recommended, and cross a mark with a horizontal bar for each film processed. The label should also include the dilution and date of preparation of the solution.

Final reminders
Apart from the advice and techniques already given for developing black and white film, here are 15 more important points to remember. There are no short cuts to good developing practices, in spite of what your friends might say. A fault on a negative will make it, at best, difficult or, at worst, impossible to obtain a good print.

Always . . .
● Wash the mixing rod and funnel after each use.
● Wash the developing tank thoroughly after use. If it is plastic use warm, not hot, water and make sure it is bone dry before use.
● Label each storage bottle clearly with chemical, dilution and preparation date.
● Make up chemicals one at a time.
● Check temperatures of stop bath and fixer—they should be within 4.5°F (2.5°C) of the developer temperature.
● Store chemicals at room temperature. Exteme cold may cause crystals of chemicals to precipitate and alter concentrations.
● Check whether the film in your camera winds on to the take-up spool emulsion-side out. If so, leave it at least 30 minutes after rewinding it back into the cassette before developing. This allows it to resume its natural curl for easy loading.
● Remove the cap from the developing tank, clockwise. It fits tightly and if you twist it anti-clockwise, you run the risk of unscrewing the whole lid and ruining the film inside the tank.
● Agitate the developing tank according to the instructions—too much or too little agitation may cause uneven development.

Never . . .
● Never clean your work area just before you use it: give the dust time to settle.
● Never let yourself become flurried—you might pick up the wrong chemical or tip a solution into the wrong bottle. Work methodically and with forethought.
● Never roll up film when it is dry: cut it into strips at once.
● Never store more than one strip of negatives in an envelope: they will scratch.
● Never leave the spring collar on the developing tank column when not in use: it will lose its grip.
● Never use clothes pegs or paper clips to hang a film: it may slip out.

Choosing the developer

There are many developers for black-and-white films in the shops. Some are liquids, others are powders. They have interesting names and numbers, but how is the photographer to choose the best one for a particular purpose?

When choosing a developer it is important to remember that films and developers go together in a partnership—think of a film/developer combination rather than of a film or a developer in isolation. The best plan is first to choose a film according to the lighting conditions and kind of result required, then pick a developer to suit the film. But don't keep changing—experiment at first, then settle down to one or two combinations which suit your kind of photography and stick to these.

Liquids or powders?

Developers are either supplied as concentrated liquids, or as powders which you dissolve. Liquid concentrates are easier to prepare and, because they are used once only (one-shot), there is no need to remember how many films have been developed in the solution. However, liquid developers cost more and are not available to suit every type of film. There is a greater range of powders which keep longer than liquids but, when made up into solution, keeping qualities are about the same.

The qualities desired of films are definition (sharpness), fine grain (no coarse texture of image) and high emulsion speed (ability to react fast to light). Developers can influence these qualities and are often classified as being 'high definition', 'fine grain', or 'high speed' types. Sometimes two desirable qualities can be combined, but most developers achieve a compromise between the different qualities. For example, making the grain finer tends to soften the definition, and so on.

There are other factors to consider. An important one is contrast (the degree of difference between light and dark areas). If a film has low inherent contrast there is little point in using a low contrast developer, because the results will inevitably look flat and dull. Similarly, if a film is grainy, as high speed films tend to be, a coarse-grain developer will exaggerate the sandpaper effect.

Developer types

Universal developers are made for use with films and papers of all types. However, like many multi-purpose products, they are not as good for particular tasks as those developers

▲ Printed from Tri-X film developed in a general purpose developer.

▼ FP4 film processed in Acufine gives good grain and tonal range.

made for a specific purpose; for the best results it is advisable to use different developers for films and papers. The most extreme fine-grain developers lose emulsion speed. You can use a fast film (for example, 400 ASA) and end up with an effective 160 ASA and the same fineness of grain as if you had started with a medium speed film in the first place. However, the quality of image from the slower film is higher than from the fast film slowed down. So if you want fine grain start with a slow (25 ASA to 80 ASA) or medium speed (100 ASA to 200 ASA) film in the first place.

High definition developers tend to give a coarse grain. They should be used only with slowish films that have fine grain to start with, so that making it coarser does not matter much. Generally, such developers are used only for special purposes where sharpness of image is extremely important. Speed-increasing developers allow a higher speed rating to be used than the one on the side of the packet. Generally, the increase is about 60% or two-thirds of a stop. For example, a 125 ASA film could be rated at 200 ASA; which is useful if, for example, you want to stop down to improve lens performance. These developers can also give either reasonably fine grain or good edge definition, or a compromise between the two, and are a good choice for everyday work. However, do not expect any developer to give you everything!

It should be remembered that speed-increasing developers do not push up the speeds of all films equally. Read the instruction leaflets with such developers before exposing the films.

Maximum speed developers are for emergency use only, when you cannot get a picture otherwise. It is only sensible to use them with fast or extreme speed films. Do not use them with slow or medium speed films because you would get better results by employing a fast film with a less extreme developer.

Developer names

Developers are sold under various names or numbers. Sometimes the name makes the manufacturer's aims clear—'fine grain' or 'high definition' would be obvious—but more often code letters and numbers are used which give few clues of type.

Most manufacturers of film suggest their own developers and these are always safe to use and work ade-

PREPARATION OF DEVELOPER SOLUTIONS—Liquid concentrates

 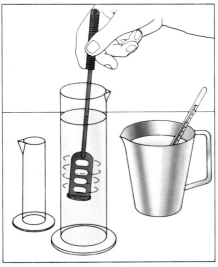

1 MEASURE CONCENTRATE
Check how much developer you need to cover the film in the developing tank. Calculate how much concentrate is required based on the dilution ratio. For small volumes it is more accurate to use a 45ml measure.

2 ADD WATER AND MIX
Transfer the concentrate to a 600ml measure. Fill a jug with water adjusted to processing temperature; rinse small measure, adding washings to large measure. Add more water from the jug to bring the solution up to the correct volume. Stir well to mix. Check the temperature before use.

POWDER DEVELOPERS

 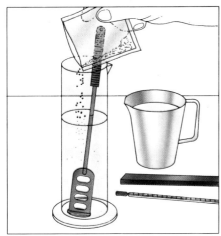

1 ADD FIRST POWDER
Powder developers usually come in two parts. Fill jug with hot water at temperature specified in instructions on package. Measure out ¾ of amount of water. Add first chemical and stir well. After stirring let the liquid settle. Check that no crystals remain undissolved either floating on top or on the bottom. (This chemical dissolves less readily.)

2 ADD SECOND POWDER
Having ensured that the first chemical is completely dissolved, add the next chemical. Stir well to dissolve it. When dissolved add cold water to bring the developer to the correct volume. Finally, stir again. Check the temperature before use.

quately. However, independent chemical firms often produce developers which can be more convenient or are better suited to some particular purpose. The table will help to show the pattern and assist in making a choice.

Characteristic curves

Another quality of developers is tone distribution. This means the way in which tones are rendered. Some developers are especially good for the middle tones (the mid-greys) and tend to squash together the dark shadow tones. Other developers may, for example, give equal emphasis to tone throughout the range. There is no need to worry unduly about this until you start becoming more familiar with chemicals and their properties and specializing in particular subjects. A quick way to see what kind of tones a developer gives with a particular film is to look at the graphs called 'characteristic curves'.

These graphs can seem mysterious at first sight, but they are quite simple. A picture can be worth a thousand words and characteristic curves are a simplified picture of the results of developing a particular film in a certain developer. Exposure is measured along the bottom of the graph and density

(blackness of the negative) in the upward direction. The sloping line shows how the tones are reproduced. The steeper the slope the higher the contrast; the flatter the slope the flatter the contrast. The bottom of the line is called the toe and the top is the shoulder. Highlights of the scene (the lightest parts) are recorded in the shoulder of the curve whereas the shadows are recorded in the toe.

If the line is reasonably straight, tones are equally spaced out. If, for example, the shoulder flattens out, then highlights would not be well separated and in a snow scene, or picture of glassware, the essential sparkle would be lacking, though this would not show with other subjects, such as a landscape. Also, the negatives would be easy to print. As you become more expert, however, the characteristic curves will mean more and give you further information; for example, if you wanted to do push processing you would be looking for developer with a long toe portion.

Paper developers

Although there are many makes the situation is remarkably simple when developing black-and-white enlarging papers. For most purposes any of the good makes will serve perfectly well.

There are powders and concentrated liquids. Again, powders are slightly cheaper but you have the trouble of making the stock solution. Do not buy too large a quantity of powder even though it is cheaper, because solutions have a limited storage life and trouble can arise if you try to use only part of the powders at a time.

There are very small differences in the image colours produced by different brands, expecially with warm-tone papers, but most photographers agree that for practical purposes it matters little which print developers you use. If a brand is reasonably economical, keeps well under your storage conditions and gives no trouble in use, then there is no reason to change. Most photographers use the ready-made liquids because they are easier to prepare.

Developers should always be stored in tightly stoppered bottles which are labelled clearly with the name of the developer and date of preparation, and whenever possible they should be kept full. And the bottles should be made of dark glass or non-porous plastic. It is possible to buy special soft-contrast print developers but it is easier, and often more satisfactory, to use a paper one grade softer than you would normally when printing that particular negative.

Characteristic curves for different film: developer combinations

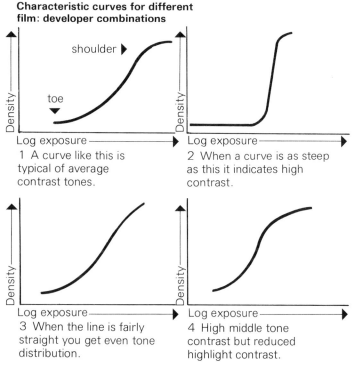

1 A curve like this is typical of average contrast tones.

2 When a curve is as steep as this it indicates high contrast.

3 When the line is fairly straight you get even tone distribution.

4 High middle tone contrast but reduced highlight contrast.

▶ **A combination of HP5 film developed in Microphen which is very good for bringing out shadow detail.**

Black and white film developers

Developer	Manufacturer	Qualities	Speed rating	Suitable film	Powder or liquid	Remarks
D76	Kodak	Good grain Fair definition	Normal	All types	Powder	Well known, general purpose negative developer
ID11	Ilford	As above	Normal	All types	Powder	As above
Microphen	Ilford	As above	About 60% extra	All types	Powder	Same general type as D76 ID11 but altered to give more speed
Promicrol	May & Baker	As above	About 60% extra	All types	Powder	As above
Aculux	Paterson	As above	About 30% extra	All types	Liquid	Can be thought of as a liquid D76
Ultrafin FD7	Besseler	As above	About 100% extra	All types	Powder	Has replenisher tablets
Ultrafin FD5	Besseler	Good sharpness Fair grain	Normal	All types	Liquid	General purpose negative developer
Unitol	Johnsons	Fair grain	Normal	All types	Liquid	Compensating type
Perceptol	Ilford	Very fine grain	Speed reduced to about 50%	All types	Liquid	Sacrifices speed for fine grain
Ultrafin FD1	Besseler	High sharpness	About 100% extra	Slow and medium	Liquid	Grain too coarse for fast films Highlights flatten
Acutol	Paterson	High sharpness	About 40% extra	Slow and medium	Liquid	Not meant for fast films
Acuspecial	Paterson	Combines sharpness and fine grain	Normal	Slow and medium	Liquid	Compensating type. Gives details in shadows and highlights but squeezes together middle tones
Definol	Johnsons	Good definition	About 30% extra	Slow and medium	Liquid	Not for fast films
Acuspeed	Paterson	Not fine grain	100% to 30% extra	Fast	Liquid	For maximum speed. Use only when you must
DK 50	Kodak	Not fine grain	Normal	Very fast	Powder	A clean working developer very suitable with Royal X Pan

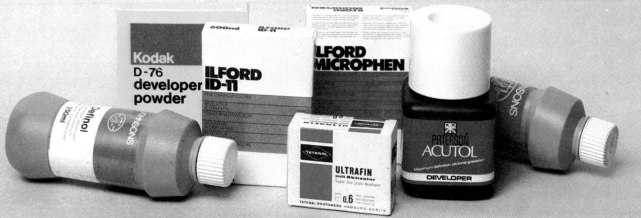

Black-and-white negative faults

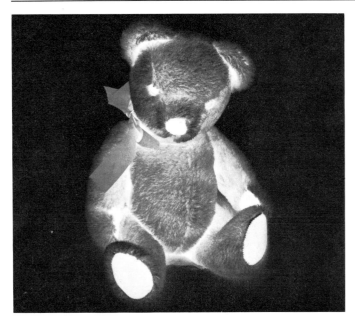

THE NORMAL NEGATIVE

A normal negative shows a full range of tones from highlights to shadows with details in both. Shadow areas and borders are free from fogging and the emulsion is clean—there are no marks or scratches.

Mistakes made during processing or while the film is in the camera account for a wide variety of negative faults. In fact, if you consider how many things can go wrong, it is a wonder that most people manage to produce such consistently good negatives.

Mistakes can happen when you take the photographs; for instance, you may inadvertently under- or over-expose the film. Or the image may be unsharp and that, too, will have happened while the picture was being taken. It could be a case of camera shake, or mean that the subject moved but, if many frames are fuzzy, there is likely to be something wrong with the camera itself.

It is, however, at the processing stage that the whole film can be ruined by faulty techniques. Most negative faults make it difficult to produce a high quality print, and at worst can make the negative a complete write-off.

Cleanliness and order

The only way to avoid damaging your films during processing is to take great care at every stage from the moment you begin to load the film into the reel. The two keys to success are cleanliness and orderliness. Make sure that all the equipment is always washed thoroughly, especially the reel on which you wind the film for processing in the developing tank. If you are using the same measure for different chemicals, wash it well after each one. Above all, keep your fingers clean; wash them after handling any chemicals, especially fixer, and dry them on a *clean* towel.

The most common faults

Under- or over-development, the most common negative faults, occur during development, which is the most critical stage of processing. Correct development depends on various factors—temperature, time, the age and dilution of the developer, and the amount of agitation. Any deviations from the recommended practice will affect the contrast of the image.

There is a lot to remember when you first begin to process your own films and mistakes are bound to happen, but don't become discouraged. What initially seems tricky soon becomes a matter of routine.

Use the guide on these pages to help you to identify some of the faults which may have occurred, and you will find that you quickly start to produce fine quality negatives without defects.

Examining the negatives

To look at and assess negatives, shine a desk lamp on to a sheet of white paper. Hold the negatives above the paper so no light falls on the front of them and use a magnifying glass to examine them in detail. First look at the image as a whole, then at the highlight (dense) and shadow (thin) areas, and finally at the borders.

The key points to look for are: shadow areas and borders free from fogging; a range of tones from highlights to shadow areas, all showing detail; and a clean appearance to the emulsion.

On a negative, the tonal values are reversed so the 'highlights' are actually the dark or dense areas which were, of course, the lightest parts in the original scene. Similarly, the 'shadow' areas are the thin or light parts of the negative, or the dark parts of the scene.

There is also a standard test which you can use to check the overall density and contrast. Place the negative emulsion-side-down on a printed page. You should just be able to read the type through the densest areas (highlights) and see a slight density in the (thin) shadow areas.

With practice you will learn to notice faults on your negatives. Contact sheets help too, but they are only an average guide to individual negatives because of the single overall exposure for printing.

There is no substitute for the real thing, so bear in mind that the negatives reproduced here in printed form lack the transparent quality and texture of an actual negative, which make it easier to assess the quality. Each negative is accompanied by its contact print to provide an indication of how it would appear printed normally, but remember that many faults won't show up very markedly until the negatives have been enlarged.

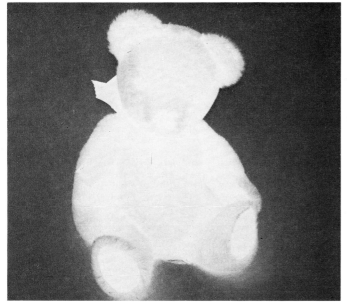

UNDER-EXPOSURE

Problem: a thin negative with blank clear shadows and though the highlights show some detail, they are greyer than normal. These are the characteristics of under-exposure.

Cause: the wrong ASA/DIN film speed (too fast), too small an aperture, too fast a shutter speed or a light reading taken from the brightest part of the scene only.
Cure: by chemical or printing means.

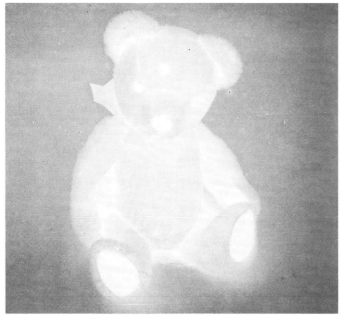

UNDER-DEVELOPMENT

Problem: a thin negative with less contrast than normal. It looks under-exposed but that causes blank shadows, whereas in under-development these areas have detail. There is a lack of highlight density.
Cause: too short a time in the developer, too cold a solution, or the use of weak or stale developer. (Faint edge numbers are a sign of stale developer.)

Cure: developer cannot work effectively at a temperature lower than 68°F (20°C) so always watch this, as well as the time, dilution and age of developer. Store developer in well-stoppered bottle to prevent deterioration.

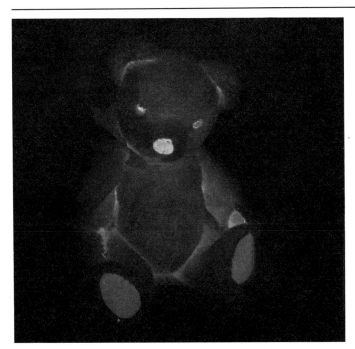

OVER-EXPOSURE

Problem: a dark, dense negative which shows some shadow detail but the mid-tones and highlights merge into a fairly even black. This is a typical sign of over-exposure.
Cause: The ASA/DIN film speed was set wrongly (too slow), the shutter speed was too slow or the aperture was too wide, or the light reading was taken from the darkest part of the scene only.
Cure: by chemical/printing means.

OVER-DEVELOPMENT

Problem: a much denser (blacker) than normal negative, like an over-exposed one. What distinguishes it, however, is a high contrast, which an over-exposed negative lacks.
Cause: too long a period in the developer or too high a temperature.
Cure: watch the timing and the temperature in future. Later chapters explain how to rectify this fault which may be modified by chemical treatment or compensated for during printing.

WHITE SPOTS

Problem: round white spots with dark edges.
Cause: air bubbles on the surface of the emulsion prevented development.
Cure: let fresh developer settle before use—tap water is often aerated. Pour developer evenly into tank and tap tank to dislodge any air bubbles. Some correction is possible by printing means and large negatives can perhaps be retouched.

STREAKING

Problem: uneven density of the image gives the negative a streaky appearance.
Cause: insufficient agitation during development led to some areas receiving more development than others. It is essential to agitate the film at least once every minute during development, especially if you use a rapid developer.
Cure: none. At best, the streaks may not be too obvious on the enlargement.

FOGGING

Problem: shadows and rebates in this negative are fogged (slightly opaque when they should be clear).

Cause: poor blackout during loading. Check the blackout carefully before removing the film from its protective wrapping. Eyes take time to get used to low light levels.

so remain in the darkroom for at least 10 minutes to see if it is light-tight.

Cure: chemical treatment may clear the shadow areas. If the fogging is slight it may not affect printing.

UNDEVELOPED STRIP AT TOP

Problem: a portion of this negative is undeveloped. (During agitation it underwent some development when the solution washed over that part of the negative.)

Cause: not enough developer in tank.

Cure: none. You may be able to crop the picture. Make certain that you use the right amount of developer in the tank for the film size.

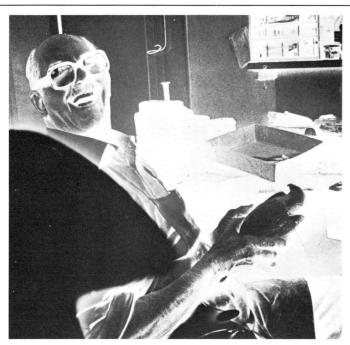

UNEVEN DEVELOPMENT AND FIXING
Problem: an unevenly developed and fixed area.

Cause: this film was badly loaded into the reel so that the emulsion on one part of the film was in contact with the back of another part of the film.

Cure: none—put it down to bitter experience. Loading requires practice so if in doubt remove the film and start again. You can often check whether the film is loaded correctly by running your finger tips over the reel tracks to feel if it has buckled or is protruding.

CRESCENT-SHAPED MARKS
Problem: crescent marks on the image.

Cause: during loading the film was kinked. It is easy to do this while you concentrate on loading it accurately into the reel and as a result it is a fairly common fault.

Cure: none. Later chapters explain how to spot out the faults on the print itself. Load film carefully, especially roll film, holding it at the extreme edges only.

NEGATIVE TOO DENSE

Problem: silver halide remains in the emulsion, 'blocking up' the shadow areas with a chemical deposit and making the whole negative much denser than it should be.

Cause: insufficient fixing. To check for correct fixing, hold the negative at a slant to the light and examine the shadows for any trace of milky greyness. It is invisible in direct light, but can be seen easily in reflected light.

Cure: refix and rewash the negatives. Your fixer may be too stale: check it with a scrap of unexposed film (for example, the tongue of a 35mm film), discard the fixer when the time to clear the film is twice that needed by fresh fixer.

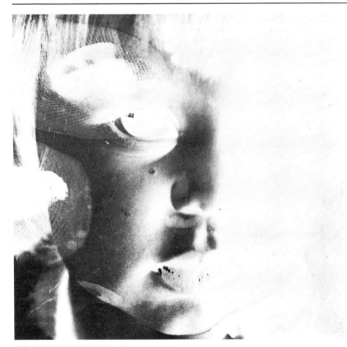

CONTAMINATION BY FIXER

Problem: fingerprints or other marks on the negative.

Cause: chemical contamination of the film, in this case from a finger splashed with fixer. Similar staining sometimes occurs along the edges of negatives and this comes from chemical contamination of the reel with fixer. Traces of fixer remained trapped in the tracks and the empty reel was not washed thoroughly enough.

Cure: normally, none. A skilled operator can sometimes 'knife-out' the black marks which appear on the print.

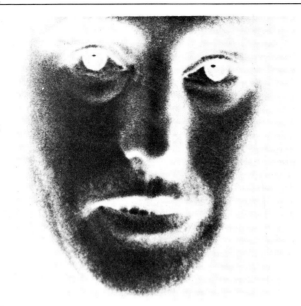

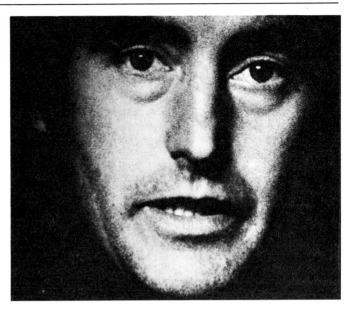

RETICULATION

Problem: a very grainy look with loss of fine detail.

Cause: the processing solutions, especially the developer or stop bath, were too hot. The gelatin which holds the silver halides expands when placed in a hot liquid then contracts suddenly when placed in another solution at a lower temperature.

Modern films are resistant to this but it can occur with excessive abuse.

Cure: none. Keep your processing solutions and final washing water within ±4.5°F (2.5°C) of the developer's temperature.

DRYING MARKS

Problem: areas of increased density across the negative.

Cause: drops of water which have dried on the emulsion cause selective intensification of the silver grains by 'clumping' them together. This is a physical change in the structure of the emulsion so rewashing will not help.

Cure: the uneven density gives small patches of lighter density on the prints which, if not excessive, could be retouched out. To avoid drying marks, always use a wetting agent and gently remove water from the film with a squeegee.

Improving your black-and-white processing

Once you have got over the initial excitement of processing and printing your first black-and-white films you will soon want to improve your techniques. Looking at the prints exhibited by your local camera club or at a photographic gallery will show the standard that can be achieved with a little practice.

The first step is to get the best possible negative. This should have an even density, be correctly exposed and developed, and display a full range of tones with detail in both highlight and shadow areas. It should also be free from dust, scratches and fingerprints.

Refining your techniques

To produce the best negatives and to get the most out of a particular developer you will need to control the processing steps carefully. The simplest way to ensure this is to adhere strictly to the processing procedure suggested by the manufacturers for each film and developer combination, provided it gives you the results you want. Most modern films have been designed to be tolerant of a great deal of variation in exposure level and processing conditions, but carelessness will still give inconsistent and unpredictable results.

Temperature control

Always check that the temperature of the developer is correct just before you pour it into the loaded developing tank. A temperature drop of as little as two or three degrees can result in lower contrast, giving flat prints unless you move to a harder grade of paper.

Try to keep the temperature of the stop bath and the fixer reasonably close to that of the developer. Although damage to the emulsion surface (called 'reticulation') caused by sudden temperature changes is rare, it *does* happen, and there is no remedy for it. (Sometimes slight reticulation can give the appearance of very coarse grain.)

Agitation

Modern developing tanks use reels that roll the film into a small space to minimize the quantity of processing solution used. Consequently the gap between the layers of film is small, and the tank must be agitated to prevent pockets of stale developer from forming, and leading to uneven development. The best way to agitate these tanks is by inversion — turn the tank upside down for a few seconds once every 30 seconds, or as

▶ **For a good quality print you need a good negative processed with care.**

specified in the instructions.

Prolonged agitation acts like an increase in developing time, and increases the density and contrast of the negative. Too little agitation decreases contrast and can also produce uneven density in the negative. Agitation must be intermittent, not constant, otherwise flow patterns can cause uneven density, especially lines from the perforations of 35mm film. Also, do not shake the tank vigorously as this causes air bubbles to form in the solution. These can produce circular marks on the negatives if not dislodged. After gentle inversion replacing the tank on the bench with a sharp tap will usually displace any bubbles that have formed.

Accuracy of timing

Time how long it takes you to empty the solution from your processing tank. Some tanks can be emptied much faster than others. If it takes five seconds, always begin pouring out the developer five seconds before the end of the development time. This will allow you to pour in the stop bath or fixer at exactly the right time to halt development.

Washing

When washing the film ensure that the water passes over the entire surface of the film. Taking the lid off the tank and putting it under the tap is not sufficient, especially with modern reels. Paterson make a Force Film Washer that directs the water to the bottom of the tank, forcing it up between the layers of film. This can also be achieved using a short length of tubing which fits down the centre of the reel.

The temperature of the wash water can be a problem in the winter. Water straight from the tap can be so cold that washing is very slow. Very cold water can also produce slight reticulation, especially if the fixer is not one with a hardener incorporated.

To overcome these problems, fill a container with water at the same temperature as the processing solution. When you have poured out the fixer, fill the tank with water from the container, and agitate. After two or three minutes, tip the water away and refill the tank from the container.

Five or six changes of water should usually be sufficient to wash the film thoroughly. You should allow a little more time for each wash, as each time the water will take longer to be contaminated by fixer.

TIPS FOR BETTER BLACK-AND-WHITE PROCESSING

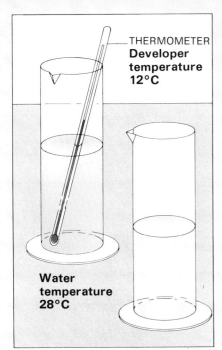

TEMPERATURE CONTROL: When diluting a solution from stock chemicals, it is quicker to use warm water than to heat working strength chemicals. For example, if a developer is formulated for use at 68°F (20°C) at 1:1 dilution, and the stock solution is eight degrees too cold (60°F, 12°C), adding an equal quantity of water that is eight degrees too warm (76°F, 28°C) will produce a solution with approximately the right temperature for processing.

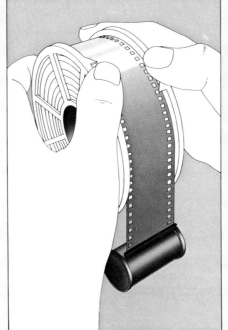

EASIER LOADING: Opening a 35mm cassette in total darkness and then attempting to feed the end of the film on to a plastic developing reel can lead to unnecessary fumbling. It is better to leave a short length of film protruding from the cassette when rewinding in the camera (usually there is a slight additional resistance before the film is completely rewound). The film end can then be trimmed to fit the reel in subdued room light and easily started in the spiral groove.

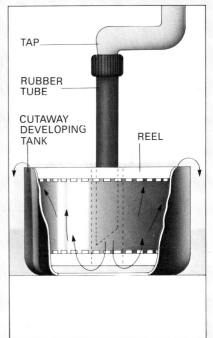

EFFICIENT WASHING: Care is needed to ensure that wash water flows from the bottom of the developing tank upwards, because fixer is denser than water and therefore tends to accumulate at the bottom of the tank. The more turbulent and forceful the water flow the better, and rubber tube attachments are available which introduce air into the flow of wash water and give the film a more thorough wash in a shorter time.

FP4 WITH DIFFERENT DEVELOPERS

Ilford FP4 film was exposed at three ASA speeds and processed accordingly.

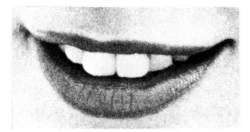

▲ **64 ASA in Perceptol gives smooth tones and fine grain (see picture, right).**

▲ **125 ASA in D-76. The standard rating gives good grain and sharpness.**

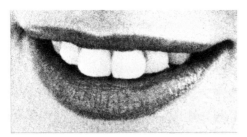

▲ **400 ASA in high energy developer. Over twice normal speed, more graininess and contrast.**

▲ **FP4 downrated to 64 ASA, developed in Perceptol: shallow depth of field and smooth tones give this portrait a flattering soft look.**

Controlling graininess

Different developers have varying effects on the image. The importance of this varies according to the size and type of film. If you are using a medium or large format, at least 2¼ x 2¼in (6 x 6cm) or greater, and only intend to produce 8 x 10in (20 x 25cm) prints, the effects of different developers on grain may hardly be apparent. With 35mm negatives, the degree of magnification needed to produce an 8 x 10in (20 x 25cm) print is at least eight times, and with selective enlargement may be far more. At such magnifications the grain structure of the negative is going to be visible in the final print.

The graininess, or granularity, of the negative is affected by three main factors:

● The film emulsion. The higher the speed of the film the larger the original grains of silver halide will be.
● The exposure. Excess exposure will increase the density and graininess.
● The developer. These can be divided into three main types: fine grain; high definition; and high energy developers.

Choosing a developer

Fine grain developers give reasonable contrast without loss of film speed and without interfering with the original fine grain characteristics of the emulsion. Examples incude such developers as D-76, ID11, HC110, Aculux and Promicrol (not available in US). They can be used with all the commonly available types of film. Portraits, which need a smooth gradation of tones to show skin textures, and soft, gentle landscapes are ideal subjects for use with this type of developer. Where finer grain is required, Perceptol can be used. Unfortunately this developer only achieves its results by sacrificing the speed of the film by about 50%, and it is often better to use a slower film with an ordinary fine grain developer.

High definition developers produce a good contrast range without increasing granularity while improving the definition, or apparent sharpness, of the image. An example which is currently available is Acutol which should only be used with films of low or medium speed for example, Panatomic-X or FP4.

The merits of this type of developer are best displayed in photographs of scenes with plenty of fine detail, such as

▲ Tri-X at 1250 ASA, developed in high energy developer: extra depth of field makes the subject sharper, the background more noticeable.

Kodak Tri-X film was exposed at three ASA speeds and processed accordingly.

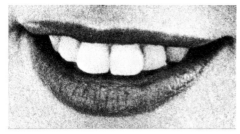

▲ 200 ASA in Perceptol. Very smooth gradation and slightly finer grain.

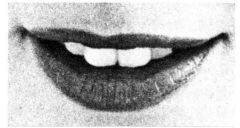

▲ 400 ASA in D-76. The standard rating gives good results for the film's speed.

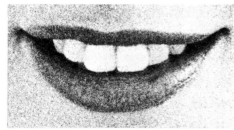

▲ 1250 ASA in high energy developer. Higher speed but extra grain (see left).

mountain scenes, or close-ups of architectural detail.

High energy developers, such as Acuspeed and Ethol Blue, produce an increase in effective speed of the film and are useful for shots taken in very low light. They are designed for use with fast films (400 ASA and over) such as Tri-X and HP5. But such developers should only be used when absolutely necessary, as the added speed is achieved at the expense of grain and definition.

Special developers for very specific purposes are no longer generally available in ready-made form. Because of a decline in sales of black-and-white materials, manufacturers have cut down the number of developers available in made-up form. However, most of the formulae have been published, so if the chemicals are available and can be measured accurately, you can make these up for yourself.

Personalized processing

Processing a film is rather like baking a cake, in that consistently good results will be obtained by following the recipe meticulously. However, as with cakes, the 'perfect' result is to some extent a matter of taste, and it is possible to vary the recipe accordingly.

For example, if your negatives seem too flat and lacking in contrast, you can increase the development time to make them more contrasty. If your negatives are too contrasty, you can decrease it. Experiment by varying film ratings, developer and development times to see how the result is affected. For example shoot a roll of 400 ASA film with the same scene exposed at ratings from 100 ASA (−2 stops) to 1600 ASA (+2 stops), then process and compare results. The best negative is the one with least density but adequate shadow detail. Repeat the process with other development times, aiming at a negative which will print on a normal (grade 2) paper as this gives you the greatest scope for variations in either direction. If you start to experiment in this way, always record the alterations you make, or you will not be able to relate causes and effects, nor repeat your results.

The pictures here show how with two common films and three developers good results can be obtained at ASA ratings from 64 to 1250. The versatility and control this allows is worthwhile.

Making contact prints

Contact prints are made by placing negatives on a sheet of light-sensitive photographic printing paper and exposing the paper to light. Where the negative is thin (in the shadow areas of the original scene) a lot of light passes through to the paper, and where it is dark (in the light areas of the original picture), less light penetrates.

This results in a positive image being formed on the paper. But, like the exposed film in the camera, the image is latent (invisible) and needs to be developed to turn it into a black and white print. Photographs printed in this way are the same size as the negatives and are usually only useful for reference.

The reasons for contacts

In the excitement of handling your own processing, it is a great temptation to bypass the contact print stage and settle straightaway for enlargements. But it is always wise to make contact prints. For one thing, it is easier to judge the merits of a particular negative from a contact print, especially if you are working with small formats like 35mm. It is impossible to judge things like facial expressions from negatives, where the tonal range is reversed. You can tell whether an image is sharp, but you need the positive print on the contact sheet to see precisely what it looks like.

Secondly, a contact print gives you the opportunity to improve the composition. The most interesting portion can be outlined with a Chinagraph pencil or China crayon as a reference for an enlargement.

Contact prints also provide an invaluable quick reference to what is on your negatives, and make filing and finding a particular subject easier.

Choosing equipment

To produce pin-sharp contact prints, it is essential to hold the negatives in firm contact with the light-sensitive surface of the printing paper. This can either be done with a contact printing frame, obtainable from a photographic shop, or, more cheaply, with a sheet of plate glass which must be heavy enough to press the negatives firmly against the paper. Working in subdued lighting makes it difficult to see as clearly as usual so, to avoid cut fingers, you should smooth down any rough edges, or you can use glass with chamfered or bevelled edges.

The normal grade of printing paper with a glossy surface (for example, Kodak grade 2 or Ilford grade 2) is recommended to start with because it can usually accommodate both flat and contrasty negatives. The glossy paper surface is also easier to mark up. With normal paper you will not get a perfect print of every frame but as you are making your contacts for reference, high quality is not vital. When you come to enlargements you may wish to try papers with different characteristics: see later section on printing papers.

An 8 x 10in (20.3 x 25.4cm) sheet of paper will take 36 frames of 35mm film and 12 frames of 2¼ x 2¼in (6 x 6cm) film, so one roll of film goes on to the same contact sheet.

White light

The white light source for exposure of the printing paper can be the light from an ordinary 40 watt frosted bulb or the light from an enlarger. If you use the 40 watt room light, check that the bulb is at least 6ft (2m) away from the printing area, to give even illumination. If you have an enlarger, raise the lamp housing until the light covers the whole sheet of paper. Close down the aperture of the lens two f stops and swivel the red filter, which acts as the enlarger's safelight, away from the lens.

The safelight

You need a light-tight room, with a coloured safelight to provide a dim working light that does not affect light-sensitive printing paper. At first, you may find it too dim, but your eyes will soon become adjusted. A safelight can either be a special bulb fitted into the light socket in the workroom, or a lamp housing with a filter, which takes a 15 or 25 watt bulb. Both types are available from photographic dealers. The colour of the filter and the wattage depends on the type of printing paper you are using. An orange bulb or filter is suitable for black and white printing.

Test your safelight

If the safelight is too close to the work area, or is the wrong colour, it will fog the printing paper. (Fogging is a reaction to light which produces an overall grey tone when the material is developed.)

To test the safelight, take a strip of printing paper and expose the emulsion side to the white light source for half the time you would use for an actual negative. Place the paper on the work bench and put two coins on top of it. Leave the coins on the emulsion side of the paper for twice the usual developing period. Then remove the coins and develop the paper. If the safelight is

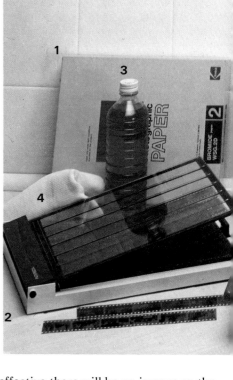

effective there will be no images on the paper, which will be universally grey.

Preparing the chemicals

Before you begin, make a preparation chart. Read through the instructions and record the amounts of developer, stop bath and fixer you need to cover one sheet of 8 x 10in (20.3 x 25.4cm) printing paper. (To assess how much of each dilution you need, fill the dish with water to a depth of ¾in (2cm) and measure the amount.) Record the dilutions for each chemical and the recommended times.

You can use the stop bath and fixer which you bought for developing film, but read the instructions carefully; dilutions may vary. However, unless you bought a universal developer to start with, you will need to get a developer suitable for black-and-white printing papers.

Temperature at the printing stage is not quite as critical as when developing the negatives, but try to hold it around 68°F (20°C). You can do this by pre-warming your diluted solutions; by standing your developing dishes in a larger dish of warm water; or with a photographic dish warmer.

When making contact prints you must put the negatives on to the paper so the

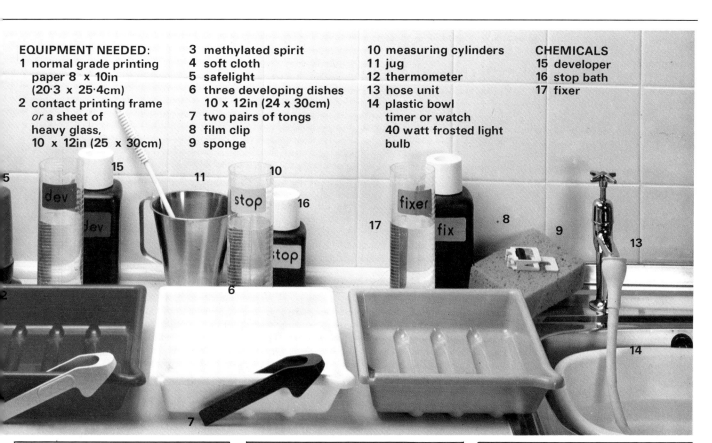

EQUIPMENT NEEDED:

1. normal grade printing paper 8 x 10in (20·3 x 25·4cm)
2. contact printing frame *or* a sheet of heavy glass, 10 x 12in (25 x 30cm)
3. methylated spirit
4. soft cloth
5. safelight
6. three developing dishes 10 x 12in (24 x 30cm)
7. two pairs of tongs
8. film clip
9. sponge
10. measuring cylinders
11. jug
12. thermometer
13. hose unit
14. plastic bowl timer or watch 40 watt frosted light bulb

CHEMICALS

15. developer
16. stop bath
17. fixer

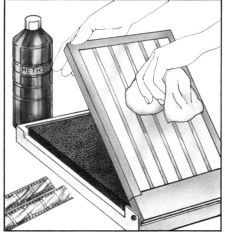

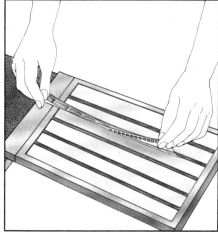

1 PREPARE THE CHEMICALS

Make up the dilutions of developer, stop bath and fixer with water at 68°F (20°C) and pour them into the developing dishes. Space the dishes so as to avoid one contaminating another with splashes. Try to maintain the room temperature at or above 68°F (20°C). After you have exposed the printing paper, check that the temperature of the developer is still 68°F (20°C) before you begin development.

2 CLEANING

Using methylated spirit and a soft, lint-free cloth, clean the glass (avoid leaving finger marks). Remove the negatives from the storage envelopes and hold them by the edges. Clean the *backs* (shiny side) of the negatives with methylated spirit on a soft cloth. Do not rub too hard. This removes drying marks and, though this is not essential for contact prints, it is for enlargements.

3 ARRANGE THE NEGATIVES

Line up the negatives in numerical order using the reference numbers on the edges. If using a contact frame, slip them into the frame, shiny side to the glass. (In new frames it may be necessary to ease up the edges of the mask gently with a blunt knife.) If you are using a sheet of glass, wait.
Now: *switch off the main light and switch on the safelight. Diagrams in orange indicate use of safelight.*

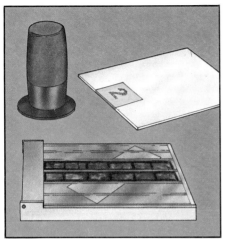

4 PUT NEGATIVES ON PAPER
Take a sheet of printing paper from the box and tear it into three strips. Replace two of the strips in the box. Keep the lid tightly closed. Put remaining strip diagonally across the printing frame. Check that the paper is glossy-side up. Lower the glass; clip it down. If using a sheet of glass put the paper on the bench; place negative dull-side down on the paper and cover with the glass, without disturbing the negatives.

5 TRIAL EXPOSURES
Switch on the white light or the enlarger. While counting up to **15** seconds, expose the whole strip to the light for **5** seconds, then block the light from a third of the test strip by holding a piece of dark card over it. At **10** seconds mask two-thirds of the strip. The remaining position has the full **15**-second exposure. Switch off the white light. The best exposure depends on your light source and this test provides the answer.

6 DEVELOP THE TEST STRIP
Check the temperature of the developer. Working under the safe-light, hold the paper strip by the edge and slip it quickly into the developer, emulsion-side up. Agitate the dish by rocking it gently for the whole of the developing time (about 2 minutes). After 20 or 30 seconds the image appears and gradually gains density. Leave it for the recommended development time. Do not worry if the image looks dark.

10 DRY THE PRINT
Remove the print, drain it and wipe the drops of water off the print with a sponge or squeegee. Dry it on clean blotting paper, or hang it up by one corner with a film clip. As it dries the print will begin to look less contrasty.

emulsion sides are together. On negatives the dull side bears the emulsion; the shiny side is the back. As a guide, negatives tend to curl with the emulsion inwards. On paper the emulsion side is glossy and also curls inwards.

Using the contact prints
Your first sheet of contact prints is dry. Now you have the pleasure of examining them closely and deciding which frames you want to enlarge.

To do this properly, you need four pieces of simple equipment: a China crayon or Chinagraph (preferably blue or yellow), a magnifying glass (the kind used for map-reading is convenient), and two pieces of L-shaped card. The size of the card depends on the negative format used, but for both 35mm and 2¼ x 2¼in (6 x 6cm) prints, masks with arms 4in (10cm) and ¾in (1.5cm) wide should be right.

First study the contacts carefully through the magnifying glass. At this stage you can immediately reject any pictures which are out of focus, ruined by camera shake or grossly under- or over-exposed. When you have selected an initial batch of frames for further consideration, use the L-shaped masks. Move them around on the print, changing the format of the picture by moving the cards. This allows you to experiment with different composition. When you have made your selection, mark in the area with the China crayon. Do this boldly so that it can be seen easily. You now have a guide for deciding how to enlarge the negatives, so saving time and printing paper when making the enlargements.

Make a filing system
Finding negatives months or years later is a daunting task unless they are correctly filed. Contact prints are best filed with the negative strips but not in the same transparent storage envelopes. This is because, unless they have been very well fixed and washed, the prints may stain and damage the negatives.

You can buy ring binders which come complete with negative storage envelopes. Then all you need to do is to attach punched, sticky strips, designed for the purpose, to the contact sheet and file it in the ring binder in front of its negatives. Index the binder and give the contact sheet and negative bag the same reference number.

▶ **When marking up contacts, a magnifying glass is useful to check fine detail.**

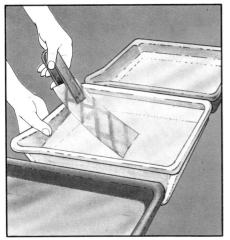

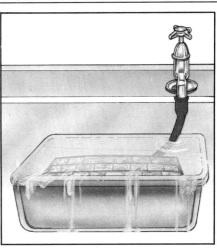

7 STOP BATH

Remove the strip from the developer. Pick up the paper by the edge with the tongs and drain it. Put the test strip into the stop bath, taking care not to let the tongs, which are contaminated with developer, dip into the stop bath. Rock the stop bath continuously. Leave the strip in the stop bath for 30 seconds. Using a clean pair of tongs, remove the strip from the stop bath and allow it to drain.

8 FIXING

Slide the test strip into the fixer and rock the dish. After 30 seconds turn on the white light. Leave the strip in the fixer for the recommended time. Take it out of the fixer. At this stage you will be able to judge the best exposure time. Return to step 4. Take a full sheet of printing paper; expose it with all the negatives for the chosen time. Then proceed through the development process as before, to this stage.

9 WASHING

To remove all traces of fixer, wash print in running water for 2 minutes (for resin coated papers) to 45 minutes (for fibre based papers). Place the print in a plastic bowl in the sink and direct the water to the bottom of the bowl through the hose unit. So clean water is introduced to the bowl while wash water overflows into the sink.

Making enlargements

Few photographers ever forget the thrill of watching the image of their first print appear in the developing tray. But there is more to printing than the technical side— it is a highly creative branch of photography. Selective enlargement of a negative can add greatly to the drama and impact of a photograph. You can make large prints from small parts of the negative, darken unwanted details and emphasize the important aspects.

It is also possible to experiment with a wide range of fascinating darkroom techniques. You can double-print two negatives, deliberately distort the perspective for special effects or even convert everyday views into unusual abstracts.

But before going on to more advanced techniques it is essential to master basic print-making procedure, which is straightforward and very enjoyable. When you look critically at the final print you may feel that parts of it appear too light and lacking in detail, while other areas may appear a bit too dark. These are quite common problems which arise when one overall exposure is given. They can be corrected by using slightly more advanced printing techniques, such as shading and burning-in. These techniques are described later.

The equipment

In addition to the basic equipment for making contact prints, you will also need the following items:
● an enlarger
● a blower brush
● a masking frame
● a focus finder

If you want to produce high gloss (glazed) prints you will also need a special drier. But if you intend to use resin-coated printing paper or matt finish paper, or let glossy paper dry normally, you won't need to have a drier because they can be left to dry by themselves. You can also manage to make enlargements without a masking frame by positioning the paper on the baseboard and securing it at the corners with small pieces of masking tape.

Choosing a printing paper

Resin-coated papers are becoming popular with many photographers because they take less time to process and dry. Fibre-based papers may be cheaper but involve more effort. While you are learning, however, it is advisable to keep using the normal Grade 2 glossy paper recommended for making the

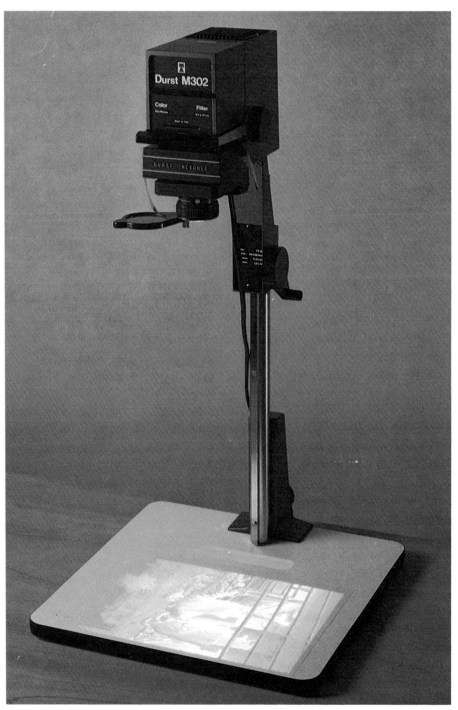

contact sheets, and perhaps to buy some hard (Grade 3) and soft (Grade 1) papers to try out. You will soon be able to tell just by looking at a negative whether it would be most effective if printed on hard, soft or normal paper. Printing papers are available in single or double weight but, unless you want to make large prints—8 x 10in (20.3 x 25.4cm), for example— single weight paper will be adequate and more economical. It is also a saving to cut 8 x 10in

Never focus through the red filter— you probably won't get a sharp focus. Only use the red filter to position the printing paper on the baseboard when you haven't a masking frame. But first focus the image on the back of a print placed on the baseboard.

(20.3 x 25.4cm) paper into quarters (use a steel rule and a very sharp knife or a rotary trimmer). While learning, you will probably want to make smaller prints. But don't forget to do the cutting by safelight. Further on this chapter gives more information on papers, such as other grades, tone, texture and special surface finishes you can choose from.

Getting ready

Follow the instructions for preparing the chemicals as explained in the previous section on making contact prints, pages 46-49. When the chemicals are ready, wash your hands and dry them thoroughly. You should *never* handle either negatives or printing paper with damp, chemically contaminated fingers.

When you use your darkroom for the first time it is a good idea to check the safelight. A too powerful bulb, or a faded safelight filter, or the wrong kind of filter for the paper being used, or a light too close to the working surface, can all result in fogging. So make a check as outlined earlier on, but this time fit a negative into the enlarger as if you were going to make a print. Give the paper an exposure of about 5 seconds. (This makes it more sensitive to light.) Don't develop the paper at once but place it on the bench, emulsion side up, with two coins on it, and leave it for about 10 minutes. Then process the paper and if circular areas of a lighter tone appear, the safelight is fogging the paper. Put in a lower power bulb, move the light further away and check that the filter is the right sort. Now test it again before proceeding.

Focusing the image

You usually compose and focus your picture with the enlarger lens fully open so that as much light as possible reaches the baseboard. So set the enlarger lens at the widest possible f number—for example, f3.5—but stop down the lens before printing. This improves the sharpness of the image and helps the lens to give the best possible definition. The smaller the f stop chosen—say, f8, f11, or even smaller—the less light will reach the baseboard.

If the negative is rather dense or the enlargement big—for example 11 x 18in (30 x 45cm)—use a stop of f5.6 or f8. A small enlargement or a thin, underexposed negative may benefit from an f stop of f11 or f16. With practice you will find it easy to select the f stop. But many photographers prefer to work with a standard stop if they can—perhaps f8 in the case of a f3.5 lens—altering the exposure rather than the stop.

It's imaginative to enlarge selectively but, if you choose a very small portion of a 35mm negative and enlarge it 15 times, there is bound to be some loss of definition.

51

1 PREPARE CHEMICALS
Dilute or mix chemicals according to maker's instructions. Temperature of developer must be over 68°F (20°C), but stop bath and fixer can be within ± 4.5°F (2.5°C) of 68°F (20°C). Pour solutions into developing trays. (Always set dishes in a row to prevent fixer contaminating the developer.) If room is cold make regular temperature checks or put solutions in storage bottles and stand in a water bath.

2 PREPARE NEGATIVE
Use contact prints to select negative and place strip on a *clean* surface. If necessary, clean the back with film cleaning fluid or meths on a soft, lint-free cloth; don't rub too hard. Remove any dust from front of negative with a blower brush. Take negative carrier out of enlarger and if fitted with glass check cleanliness. Remove marks with cleaning fluid or meths on a cloth and dust with a blower brush.

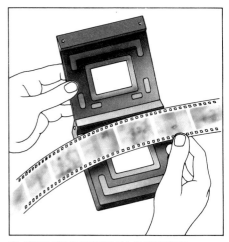

3 PUT NEGATIVE IN CARRIER
Insert the negative, emulsion side down, in the carrier, make a final check for dust, and replace the carrier in the enlarger. Switch off the light.
You will be working by safelight from now on, which is indicated in diagrams by an orange background.

Making the test strip

To make a test strip, cut a strip of paper about 2in (5cm) wide from the sheet size on which you intend to make the final print. Focus the image on the baseboard, stop down, and then, using the red swing filter if necessary, position the test strip before making the exposures. (Place it so that you get a representative section of the image.) You will also need a sheet of opaque card slightly larger than the paper.

Exposures

Block the light from consecutive sections along the strip as the exposure proceeds; zones showing the effects of different exposures are then obtained. The length of each step in the test strip exposure will vary according to the degree of enlargement, the overall density of the negative and the f stop chosen. With experience it will be easy to estimate. It should, however, never be less than 2 seconds or more than 10 seconds. An average initial exposure time is 5 seconds. While it is best to use a timer, you can simply count—one-and-two-and—and so on.
To expose the test strip, turn on the enlarger and start counting from 1 to 25 seconds. At 5 seconds cover a fifth

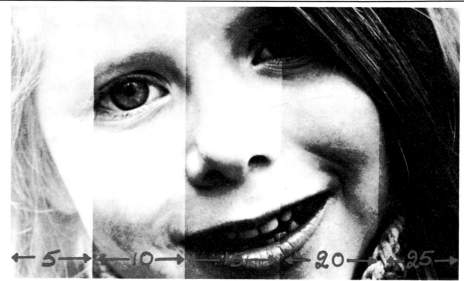

of the strip with the card. (Be careful not to move the strip; hold the card about 1in (3cm) above it.) At 10 seconds cover two-fifths of the strip, at 15 seconds, three-fifths, and so on. Switch off the enlarger at 25 seconds. You now have a test strip showing 5, 10, 15, 20 and 25 second exposures.
Process the test strip and decide which is the best exposure. If the whole strip looks too light, repeat by increasing

Here you can see that the correct exposure is around 17 seconds. To select it accurately do another test strip for 15, 16, 17 and 18 seconds.

all the exposures or open the lens by one f stop—that is, go from f8 to f5·6 and repeat the test strip procedure. If the whole strip looks too dark either decrease the exposure times or close down the lens by one stop.

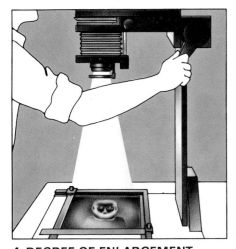

4 DEGREE OF ENLARGEMENT
Switch on the enlarger.
If you have an easel, use the white painted surface as a screen for the image. If not, use a sheet of white card or the back of a print placed on the baseboard. Raise or lower the enlarger head until the correct degree of enlargement is reached.

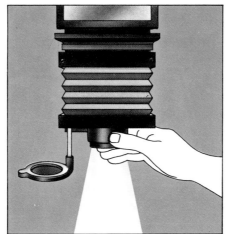

5 FOCUSING
Compose and focus the image with the enlarger lens fully open—for example, f3·5. Then stop down—for example, to f8. Turn the focusing control to and fro to focus the image sharply. Check focus by looking carefully at the image, but if making a big enlargement or if the image is very dense use a focus finder (you may want to use one in any case). Having set up the enlarger, switch off or move the red filter over the lens.

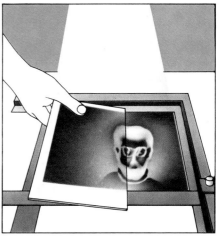

6 MAKE A TEST STRIP
Make a test strip to find the best exposure for the negative. A full explanation of how to do this is given on the page opposite.
Having made the exposures, switch off the enlarger and develop the test strip, following the method outlined in steps 8, 9 and 10. Decide which is the best exposure.

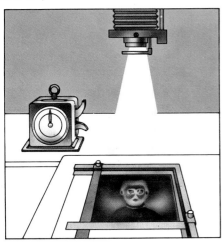

7 EXPOSE ENLARGEMENT
Take a sheet of paper from the pack. Close the pack tightly. Place the paper, emulsion side up, in the easel. If fixing it to the baseboard with masking tape you will need to swing the red filter across the lens, and switch on the enlarger to see where to position the paper exactly. Then switch off the enlarger and swing the red filter away. Wait 10 seconds, switch on enlarger and begin timing chosen exposure. Then switch off the enlarger.

8 DEVELOPING
Raise the front of the developing dish slightly. Hold paper by edge and quickly slip it into developer, shiny side up. At same time straighten dish so developer washes quickly over paper. Rock dish gently so whole of paper gets a supply of fresh solution. Develop for full time recommended—usually 2 minutes.

9 STOP BATH
At end of development lift the print from developer with tongs. Hold it by the edge. Pull it out over the edge of the developing dish so that as much developer as possible flows back into the dish. Drop print into stop; be careful not to let tongs become contaminated with stop. Gently rock stop bath. Leave print in stop for 30 seconds.

10 FIXING
Remove print from stop bath with tongs and place in fixer. Be sure it is fully submerged. Rock dish for 20 seconds so solution does its job thoroughly.
If using ordinary hypo, after 60 seconds you can turn on light but check first that all unexposed printing paper is tightly sealed up. Using rapid fixer light can be turned on after 20 seconds. Fix for recommended time.

11 WASHING THE PRINTS
If making more than one print, collect them together in a dish of water (not in the fixer) and wash all at once. The washing must be timed from the moment the last print goes into the wash. Use a dish with sink siphon to ensure prints do not stick together and wash in running water. RC papers need about 4 minutes wash, fibre papers 45, according to maker's instructions. Move prints about during this time.

12 DRYING
Blot surplus water off both back and front of print with a clean, damp sponge. You can then hang them up by the corner or lay them face up on a sheet of photographic blotting paper. Or you could use a print drier which is fast and keeps the print flat.

Glazing fibre-base papers
If you leave glossy paper prints to dry normally they will have a semi-lustre look. But this type of paper can be given a high gloss by drying it on a chrome glazing plate.

Using a drier: the secret of making good high gloss prints is a *thoroughly* clean chrome plate. Before you start, clean the chrome plate with soapy water, dry it and then rub it with methyl alcohol (meths) on a clean cloth. To gloss the print add a few drops of wetting agent to the final wash water so that it is evenly wet, remove the print from the water, drain off the excess water, and quickly place the print face-down on the chrome plate.

Use a clean flat squeegee or a print roller to press the print to the chrome plate, moving it across in one continuous movement to expel all the water and air. It is important that there are no air bells (bubbles) under the paper, which blotch the surface.

Place the plate with the prints in the drier. Use a moderate heat. When the prints are ready (after 5 minutes or so), they will unstick themselves from the chrome surface. Don't try to pull them clear sooner—you will damage the emulsion and ruin the print.

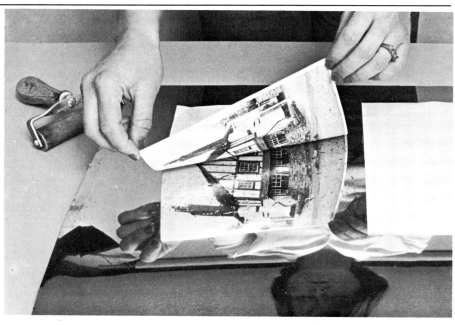

Prints sometimes refuse to come unstuck, because of grease on the plate. To free them, soak the plate and prints in hot (not boiling) water, containing a few drops of wetting agent.

Without a drier: an excellent high gloss can be achieved without a drier by leaving the print to dry on the chrome plate, or you can use a spotlessly clean

Hold the paper with both hands above the glazing plate, emulsion side down. Lay one side down first, then slowly lower the other.

sheet of plate glass. Clean the glass with methyl alcohol (meths) and then with french chalk (talcum powder), removing the chalk with a cloth.

CHOOSING THE RIGHT GRADE OF PAPER

Hard negative

Normal negative

Soft negative

Grade 1 paper **correct**

Grade 1 too soft

Grade 1 far too soft

Grade 2 too hard

Grade 2 paper **correct**

Grade 2 too soft

Grade 3 far too hard

Grade 3 too hard

Grade 3 paper **correct**

Dealing with print faults

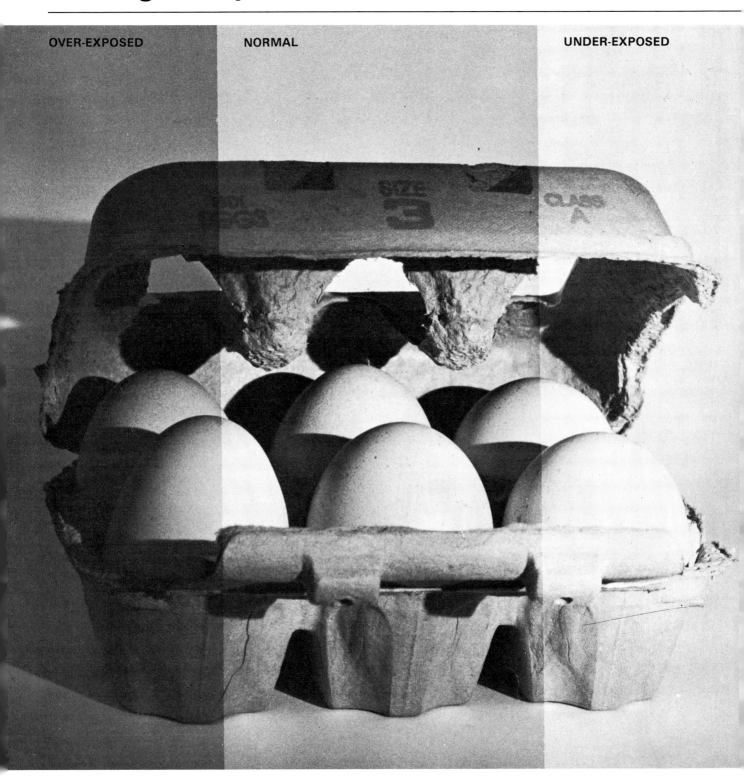

OVER-EXPOSED NORMAL UNDER-EXPOSED

In the early stage of learning any new skill, no matter how careful you are, a few mistakes are inevitable. Even the most experienced photographic processor can occasionally find that he has produced a dud print which is quickly consigned to the waste bin.

So, having keenly anticipated the appearance of a perfect print, you should be prepared for an occasional failure. By finding out what went wrong and correcting the error, you can use such disappointments to help teach yourself better techniques.

Some typical faults are shown here as a guide. Compare them with your efforts to discover what went wrong and how to ensure that you don't make the same mistake twice! After you have acquired some experience and mastered the basics of printing, white spots on the print, caused by dust and hairs on the negative, are probably the most common fault.

Fault: print looks too dark.
Cause: probably over-exposure.
Prevention: reduce the exposure time unless it is already below 5 seconds. In this case stop down by one f stop—for example, f8 to f11—and repeat test exposure. If the exposure correction doesn't work check development time and temperature; developer works more quickly at over 68°F (20°C).

Fault: print looks too light.
Cause: probably under-exposure but perhaps under-development.
Prevention: increase the exposure time unless this is already more than 60 seconds. If this is the case, open up by one f stop—that is, f8 to f5.6—and repeat test exposure. If this doesn't work check the development time and temperature. At below 68°F (20°C) developer works more slowly.

Fault: image is too flat. There is no sparkle in the highlights and no really black shadows.
Cause: the paper is too soft or the developer may have been too cold, or the development time too short.
Prevention: use a harder grade of printing paper. For example, if you used Grade 2 try a print on Grade 3 and keep a close watch on development time and the temperature of the developer.

Fault: image is too contrasty. The highlights and shadows lack detail, giving the print a soot and whitewash appearance.
Cause: the paper is too hard.
Prevention: use a softer grade of paper. For example, if you used Grade 2 try a print on Grade 1.

Fault: overall lack of contrast and grey veiling. (Only half picture is fogged—the other half is normal to show the effect.)
Cause: fogging from unsafe safelight or other source.
Prevention: check the blackout effectiveness of the darkroom and check the safelight as described in the section on making contact prints.

Fault: white finger prints or other white marks.
Cause: contamination of paper by fixer.
Prevention: make certain your hands are clean before touching any paper; wash and dry them carefully after touching fixer. Use print tongs to avoid contamination.

Fault: print is darker in the centre than at the edges.
Cause: uneven exposure owing to an incorrectly positioned enlarger lamp.
Prevention: readjust the light bulb and check the position by projecting white light on to a sheet of white paper and inspecting the density. A poorly positioned lamp will be bright in the middle and dimmer at the edges.

Fault: image unsharp all over. (Check any dust spots—even if the negative is unsharp, dust spots should be in sharp focus.)
Cause: faulty focusing in enlarger.
Prevention: first check the sharpness of the negative, then check the focus of the projected image, preferably with a focus finder. If it persists the lens may be faulty so have it checked professionally. Also the focusing device may be slack, so that the position of the lens alters slightly after focusing.

Fault: small white spots and squiggles.
Cause: dust on the negative or the negative carrier or the paper.
Prevention: some dust spots are almost inevitable if printing in dusty surroundings and they can be spotted out. But they are best eliminated by carefully cleaning the negative and carrier glass.

Fault: dark lines round edge of paper.
Cause: fogging. The unexposed paper was not properly wrapped up or exposed to stray light in the darkroom.
Prevention: check that the paper is carefully rewrapped after use and store it in a dry, dark place. Never take a sheet out of the pack until ready to expose.

Fault: multiple image with a blur in one direction.
Cause: enlarger head moved during exposure or the masking frame was inadvertently knocked.
Prevention: wait until any vibration in the head has died down before you make the exposure. Avoid moving about the darkroom while making the exposure. If traffic vibration is suspected try damping this by placing the enlarger on a thick rubber mat.

Fault: partial lack of sharpness.
Cause: the negative was not lying flat in the carrier. Also, too much heat may cause the negative to rise in the middle, pulling in the edges and blurring the image at this point.
Prevention: position negative more carefully in the carrier. Try using a glass carrier. Don't let the negative get too hot.

Black-and-white printing papers

Unless you are very careful when buying and using black-and-white printing papers, making your own black-and-white prints can be more expensive than having colour prints made by a photo-finisher. The price of the silver in black-and-white paper increases all the time. Two boxes of 100 sheets of 8 x 10in (20 x 25cm) paper can cost as much as some camera lenses. You cannot afford to make several trial prints or to guess at printing exposures, and money is wasted if you buy paper that you do not use.

Resin-coated or fibre-based?

If you have not yet started printing, you can choose between stocking up with the popular resin-coated (RC) papers or with the traditional fibre-based types. This choice will determine not only the equipment you will need for washing and drying the prints, but also how long it takes you to make each print.

RC papers have a base which does not absorb water. Only the surface layer of light-sensitive emulsion becomes saturated with processing chemicals. As a result, these papers use less chemicals, carry less of one solution over to the next, and can be washed and dried very quickly. All processing operations are shorter.

Fibre-based papers have a very absorbent card or paper base. They take longer to process than RC papers, and because they trap fixer salts in the fibre of the base, need to be very well washed after the print is developed. Washing can take over an hour in running water.

Because RC papers can be processed so easily, they are very widely used. However, they are more expensive than most fibre-based papers. In addition, they will not last as long as a properly processed fibre-based print, and do not give quite as high a standard of print quality. For most purposes the differences are small.

Paper sizes

Buying many paper sizes wastes money. You should buy the largest size you normally use. Most people choose 8 x 10in (20 x 25cm). This can easily be handled and cut down with a small rotary trimmer to smaller print sizes. If you use a 35mm camera, the negative proportions will not fit the paper, but you can trim each sheet and use the off-cuts for making test strips. Alternatively, you can crop the negative when you make the enlargement, al-

though this means that you will have to enlarge the negative slightly more to fill the paper. This will increase the graininess of the print.

Other paper sizes are better suited to the proportions of 35mm negatives if you do not want to make a test strip for every print. The larger 11 x 14in (27.9 x 35.5cm) size can be cut into two 7 x 11in (17.8 x 27.9cm) sheets, for example. When a 35mm negative is printed full-frame on a 7 x 11in (17.8 x 27.9cm) sheet, only a narrow ½in (1.25cm) strip at the end is wasted. 8¼ x 11¾in (21 x 29.7cm) paper—known as A4 size in some countries—has similar advantages but is less widely available.

Bases and surfaces

Resin-coated papers usually only come in one base weight. This is because RC paper has little tendency to curl. Fibre-based paper is softer, influenced by atmospheric moisture, and needs a heavier base if it is to lie flat without being mounted. So double weight and single weight fibre-based papers are available. Choose the former for top quality prints and larger sizes, the latter for proofs and small prints.

The most commonly used paper surfaces are glossy, lustre, semi-matt, pearl and silk. Glossy RC papers dry to a shiny finish naturally, but glossy

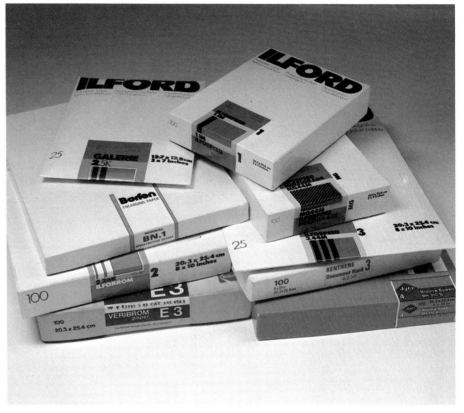

▲ The variety of printing papers can be confusing. All can give good results if exposed and processed properly.

▶ Choosing the right paper can make all the difference to your prints. For a top quality negative, only the best is good enough. This picture by *John Swannell* was printed on Ilfobrom doubleweight fibre-based paper. The glossy surface was allowed to dry naturally to an unobtrusive finish.

fibre-based papers need to be ferro-typed (glazed) to achieve a very smooth surface. The finish of an unglazed glossy fibre-based paper is liked by many photographers, and Ilford RC Pearl surface resembles this. Lustre has a coarse texture which breaks up reflections from the paper surface and hides grain. Silk has a regular fabric-like texture. Semi-matt shows fine detail well but can look too dead for some pictures. True matt surfaces are only found on fibre-based papers.

Contrast

In order to cope with a variety of negatives, printing papers are made in a range of contrast grades. There are two types—papers in set grades, where each grade is sold in a separate package, and variable contrast papers which

▲ The surface of the paper you choose for prints can completely change the look of the picture. From left to right: *Glossy* gives the best contrast between shadow and highlight, but can reflect light annoyingly. *Matt* paper cannot give such rich shadows; and the texture of *silk* paper will not suit all subjects.

cover all grades with one paper.

Most negatives will print well on grade 2 or the grades immediately above and below it on the scale. The more extreme grades such as grade 0 (soft) and grade 4 (hard) are used to correct for negative faults.

To cover all possibilities with seperately graded paper, you will need to buy boxes of grades 1, 2 and 3, and smaller packets of the more extreme grades.

Variable contrast papers such as Ilfospeed Multigrade and Kodak Polycontrast solve the problem of buying all these grades. One paper covers the whole range, with coloured filters in the enlarger controlling the print contrast. With Ilfospeed Multigrade, yellow filters make the print less contrasty, while magenta filters increase the contrast. There are seven filters altogether, giving more evenly spaced grades than equivalent individually graded papers. Multigrade paper at its highest contrast is not quite as hard as a conventional grade 5 paper, however.

Processing

RC and fibre-based papers need slightly different types of chemicals, though prints made on one type of base can

GRADED PAPER CONTRAST RANGE

▲ The range of contrast grades available with individually graded papers is wide. Here Ilfospeed grade 0 has given a flat, dead-looking print from this negative. This is the softest plastic-based paper in Ilford's range.

▲ Grade 3 is much closer to the correct contrast grade for this negative. Grade 3 and grade 2 are the grades you are likely to need for the majority of your negatives and are therefore the ones you will use most.

▲ Grade 5 is too contrasty for most negatives—prints on this grade will usually be too stark and lacking in detail. If you really need extreme contrast, even harder grades are available on fibre-based paper.

usually be developed in chemicals intended for the other. Chemicals for fibre-based papers are usually slightly cheaper than those for RC papers. RC paper developers give richer tones, better blacks, and shorter developing times when used with the papers for which they are designed.

Ilfospeed Multigrade has it own developer. With some other developers, the image colour may change slightly with different contrast settings. If you burn-in part of a picture at a different contrast setting from the rest this change will be noticeable.

Some developers are intended to give different image tones to prints, so that you can choose between warm-toned, neutral and cool-toned prints without having to stock special papers.

Whatever developer you use, make sure you follow the maker's temperature and development time recommendations carefully. Most fibre-based papers need a stop bath between developer and fixer to prevent the fixer from being contaminated by developer carried over by the print. RC papers also need a stop bath because they can stain badly if fresh developer on the print surface comes into contact with the fixer.

Nearly all fixer solutions are based on ammonium thiosulphate and work quickly. Fresh fixer will treat a print in 30 seconds. When fixer activity has slowed to take 2 to 3 minutes, it is time to discard the fixer. You can check how rapidly your fixer works by timing how long a piece of scrap film leader takes to clear in the fixer dish.

Alternatively, there are some commercial solutions available for testing fixer. With RC papers, a hardening fixer may slow down drying and demand longer wash times, but the print will be less sensitive to scratching and finger marks when dry. Older hypo-based fixers need 5-10 minutes treatment time, but are not advisable unless extreme economy is important. The temptation to turn the lights on before fixing is complete is too great with longer fixing times.

Storage

If you intend to keep a large stock of paper, you should make sure that it does not deteriorate before you can use it all up. Unexposed paper is best stored in a cool, dry place. A cupboard away from sources of heat such as radiators or windows is suitable. Make sure that your paper is out of reach of

children, who may find the temptation to open the boxes to see what is inside irresistible.

Points to watch

● Try to match the sizes of paper you keep in stock to your negative size and to your usual degree of enlargement. Unless you particularly like the effect, making prints with wide unexposed borders is a waste of paper and processing chemicals.

● Try to expose and develop your films so that most of your negatives can be printed on grade 2 or grade 3 paper. It is less trouble (and gives better results) to control your negative processing carefully than to stock large amounts of very hard and very soft paper to deal with difficult negatives.

● Use chemicals that are suitable for the paper you are using. Best results are usually given by following manufacturers' recommendations.

When you start making your own prints, you will probably need a variety of different papers and chemicals to experiment with. But as you gain skill and adopt your own printing style, you will settle down with those papers and chemicals that give you the best results for your type of pictures.

USING VARIABLE CONTRAST PAPER

FILTER 1

The major advantage of variable contrast paper is that only one box of each sheet size need be stocked. This advantage is usually sufficient to outweigh the minor disadvantages of the paper:— the range of contrast available is not as great as from individually graded papers, changes in grades require recalculation of printing times, and the paper is only available on a RC base. Left: the softest grade obtainable on Ilford's Multigrade paper. Below left: a normal grade produced by printing through filter 4. Below right: filter 7—the hardest grade. For most purposes this range is sufficient. The range of intermediate grades is useful for experienced printers. Other possibilities include varying the contrast of different parts of the print by burning-in with filters.

FILTER 4

FILTER 7

Using variable contrast paper

Variable contrast printing papers offer many advantages to both amateur and professional photographers. The biggest of these is that it enables you to make high quality prints from almost any negative using only one type of paper and a set of filters, instead of using several different grades of paper. This means significant savings in cost, because there is no need to buy several packets of different grade paper which may rarely be used.

How they work

Most papers for printing black and white negatives consist of a base material coated with a layer of emulsion sensitive to bluish coloured light. Modern variable contrast paper, on the other hand, has an emulsion which is partly sensitive to blue light and partly to green light. The blue sensitive component produces a high contrast image while the green sensitive component produces a lower contrast image.

This means that if just the blue sensitive component of the emulsion is exposed, the result is a contrasty print. If just the green sensitive part is exposed the print will be soft. By varying the proportion of blue and green sensitive emulsion exposed, you can produce print contrasts between the two extremes, thus controlling the final contrast of the print very precisely indeed.

You can control the colour of the light reaching the paper by using filters either under the enlarger lens or in the filter drawer above the negative carrier. Filters are available that are suitable for use in either position. Yellow filters, which absorb blue light, give a less contrasty image, while magenta filters, which absorb green, will increase print contrast.

Filters vary from manufacturer to manufacturer. In the United States, Kodak produce a range of variable contrast papers on different weights of fibre and resin coated (RC) bases. However, these papers are not widely distributed in other parts of the world. Ilford's Ilfospeed Multigrade is a variable contrast paper that is widely available.

Additionally, Ilfospeed Multigrade is a newer product that gives a greater range of contrast than other brands of variable contrast paper. For many uses, this outweighs the disadvantage that Multigrade is only available on a RC base.

Ilford supply a calculator with their set of filters that enables you to determine the correct exposure when you change

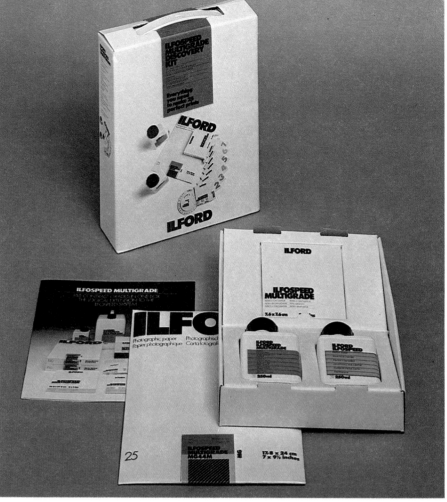

from one filter to another. This is necessary because the effective speed of the paper varies according to the amount of low or high contrast emulsion exposed by the magenta or yellow filters. The Ilford calculator is easy to use. If the print you make has the right density but the wrong contrast, turn the calculator dials until the filter number used is next to the exposure time, then read off the correct exposure against the filter number you will use for the next print.

Kodak publish tables of effective speeds for their Polycontrast variable contrast papers. The Kodak Black and White Darkroom Dataguide includes a calculator dial that can be used with these speeds in a similar way to the Ilford calculator. Alternatively, new exposure times can be worked out for both Ilford and Kodak papers by multiplying the effective printing speed of the first filter used by the exposure time, then dividing by the effective printing speed of the new filter. The ANSI system of

printing paper speeds is becoming more and more widespread among paper manufacturers, and allows the speeds of different brands and types of paper to be directly compared.

Using a colour head

If you have an enlarger with a colour mixing head, you can use it to control the contrast of variable contrast papers. However, you will probably find that you will need a supplementary magenta filter to achieve the highest contrast of which the paper is capable. Typical colour head settings for Ilford Multigrade paper are given in the accompanying table, but note that although these settings will give equivalent contrasts to those of the Ilford Multigrade filters, the Multigrade exposure calculator cannot be used to work out new exposure times. This is because the Multigrade filters incorporate neutral density dye to bring the speed of the paper at different contrast settings into a logical sequence.

ORIGINAL PRINT

LOW CONTRAST PRINT

HIGH CONTRAST PRINT

▲ Since nearly all modern enlargers have a built-in filter drawer, changing print contrast is simple. Low contrast, above right, requires a yellow filter, while high contrast, right, is given by magenta filtration. Average contrast, above, is given when no filters are used.

◀ If you have not tried variable contrast paper, you should. Products like the Ilford Multigrade Discovery Kit, shown here, provide a convenient introduction to the system. Photographers who usually print their pictures on resin coated graded paper usually find that there are advantages to be gained from switching to variable contrast paper. The quality of resin coated variable contrast paper is about the same as that given by other RC papers, but the versatility of the material is much greater. The only extra equipment necessary is a set of filters and a simple dial-type calculator to work out exposure times. Both are included in the Multigrade Discovery Kit.

Photographers who do a lot of black and white printing on variable contrast paper may find it worth using a special head on their enlarger with the necessary filters built in. The Ilford Multigrade 400 is a typical unit. It contains two lamps, one with a yellow filter, one with a magenta filter. By varying the strength of the two lamps, with an electronic control unit, any contrast grade can be produced. The Multigrade 400 is made in two models to fit large and small enlargers. Similar light sources are also available from other manufacturers for use with both Ilford and Kodak variable contrast papers.

Making your prints

The best method to use when you start to make prints on variable contrast paper is to make your first print with no filter. This will produce a print of similar contrast to one on a grade 2 conventional paper. If this first print is much too contrasty or much too soft, make another print with a different filter.

COLOUR FILTER EQUIVALENTS TO ILFORD MULTIGRADE FILTERS

	Yellow filters		Magenta filters				
Multigrade filter numbers	1	2	3	4	5	6	7
CC values (Kodak, Paterson, Unicolor filter sets and many colour heads)	45	30	15	50	75	100	170
Durst, Rollei, and some European colour heads	30	20	10	33	50	66	113
Agfa filter sets	60	40	20	66	100	133	227

These filter values will be correct for most sets of colour filters and colour heads; however, since different enlarger manufacturers have different calibration scales on their colour heads, and since individual colour filters fade with use, you should experiment to make sure that these values are correct for your equipment. You will also need to experiment to find the proper exposure time for each contrast setting. The exposure will vary from that given by variable contrast calculators.

When you have produced a print which has the correct density and contrast, use this filtration value as the starting point for prints from other negatives.

In the long term you will find it easier if your negatives can be printed on unfiltered variable contrast paper. While you will always find that there are some negatives that need extra filtration, it is possible to make most of your negatives print well on unfiltered variable contrast paper by adjusting your negative development times. The times given by manufacturers should be regarded as a guide. Your lenses, metering technique and enlarger will all influence the degree of development necessary for your negatives. If you find that your negatives all need a high contrast filter, you should develop future rolls of film for a little longer than the recommended time. If your negatives are too contrasty and need a low contrast filter, reduce the development time until you have fine-tuned your negative development precisely. You may need to adjust the ASA setting of your light meter as well as your development time. If your negative exposure and development technique is consistent, most of your negatives will then print satisfactorily with no filtration.

Processing

Processing variable contrast papers is not very different from processing normal black and white printing papers. It is best to use the paper developer recommended by the manufacturer, since the wrong developer may sometimes cause unevenness in image tone if different parts of the print are made with different contrast filters.

Ilfospeed Multigrade is intended to be part of a rapid-processing black and white printing system, and Ilford, therefore, make special chemicals to process this RC paper. Ilfospeed Multigrade developer is a concentrated liquid which is diluted with 9 parts of water for use. It gives short developing times, with the image appearing in 10 seconds and developing fully in a minute at 68°F (20°C). Other print developers can be used, although ordinary Ilfospeed developer is not recommended. Development time will need to be extended to 2 minutes if Ilfospeed Multigrade developer is not used.

Any normal stop bath and non-hardening fixer can be used with Ilfospeed Multigrade. Fixing takes only 30 seconds. A 2 minute wash in running water is enough to remove traces of fixer afterwards.

Creative control

Because you can produce a wide range of different contrasts on variable contrast paper by using different filters, you can, with experience, produce different grades on the same sheet of paper. For example, you can print the foreground of a picture through one filter and the sky through a different one.

You might wish to do this if you have a low contrast foreground and a high contrast sky. The technique is to first of all expose the whole negative through a filter giving a high contrast image. Make the exposure long enough to give the foreground enough density in the final print. Then expose the sky area through a low contrast filter while shading the foreground with your hand or a piece of card. The result is a print which has good gradation in both the sky and the foreground. It can be extremely difficult, or even impossible, to achieve such effects with simple burning and dodging methods on graded printing paper.

▶ **Making a high quality print is a matter of skill and judgement. Variable contrast paper can make it easier to achieve the effects you want from your negatives.** *John Swannell*

MIXING YOUR GRADES IN A SINGLE PRINT

▲ A sunny day, a white-painted house, and a shady path. The result is a picture that combines under- and over-exposure on the same negative. The foreground is under-exposed and lacks contrast, while the house is over-exposed and too contrasty. The result is a negative which is hard to print.

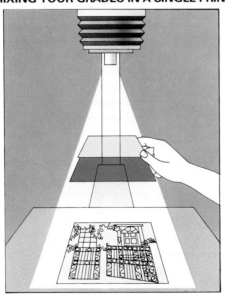

▲ The remedy is local contrast control with variable contrast paper. In this case, the top half of the print needs a yellow filter for a soft gradation, while the lower half needs hard magenta. The two filters can be held in the light path projected by the enlarger to give the desired result.

▲ Although the filters are of varied densities and give different effective paper speeds, it is often not necessary to adjust printing times to compensate. It is usually the thin parts of the negative that need to be printed at a slower but higher contrast filtration. This print was made with one exposure.

Printing controls

Although you are probably quite satisfied with your prints as a rule, there may be times when they don't quite come up to your expectations; there may be areas which print darker than you want or highlights which burn out (are too pale and lack detail). In these cases you can improve the results considerably by controlling the exposure locally. This is called shading or dodging (making an area lighter) or burning-in (making an area darker). Shading or dodging is also referred to as 'holding back'. Other controls include flashing, to reduce the contrast of a print and improve highlight detail; correcting distortion such as converging verticals; and, in colour prints, correcting the colour balance locally. (You can also dodge, shade, burn-in and correct verticals on colour prints, but you cannot flash colour papers.)

Dodging tools

Quite a lot of shading and burning-in can be done with nothing more elaborate than your hands. For example, if you want to darken the sky in a landscape, simply hold your hand so that it casts a shadow over the land part of the picture but lets the sky receive extra exposure.

And if you want to burn in, say, a window in an interior shot to give added detail you can, with a little practice, form your hands into a cup shape so that just the area of the window receives extra exposure. But a few simple tools will make the task easier. One or two companies manufacture them but they are easy to make. All you need are two or three pieces of black card cut into geometric shapes and attached with tape or staples to thin, stiff wire—such as bicycle spokes or florist's wire. (The wire has no appreciable effect as it is moved constantly.) The shapes should be a circle, a triangle, and so on—make them in several sizes—and one piece of wire with a small wad of cotton balls on the end is particularly useful. You can tease the cotton balls into all sorts of shapes which will enable you to shade areas such as a tree.

Pieces of card with holes in them are useful for burning-in small areas. Again, make several with different shaped holes in them. Ideally, the card should be black on one side and white on the other. You can then hold it with the white side uppermost, so that you can see the image, while the black underside prevents light being reflected back on to the printing paper and degrading the highlights of the print.

When you use dodging tools, the important thing to remember is to keep them moving in a random pattern—round and round, back and forth and so on—all the time. This prevents hard lines forming in the areas you have been shading or burning-in, caused by the edges of the shadow cast by the dodger on the printing paper.

Shading and burning-in

The best position for dodgers for shading or burning-in is about a third of the way up from the baseboard of the enlarger to the lens. If you hold the dodger too near the lens the shadow cast will be too soft around the edges and it will be difficult to control the dodging accurately. On the other hand, if you hold the dodger too near the baseboard the shadow will tend to have hard edges and you'll need much larger dodgers for any given area.

Of course, if you want to dodge areas of different shapes from your dodging tools, you can tilt the dodger to form a modified shape. A round dodger, for instance, will form an elliptical shadow when tilted, while a square shape when tilted will form a rectangle.

The test strips you make to establish the overall correct exposure will also help you to decide how long you need to burn-in or shade an area. Perhaps the test strip of a landscape indicates an overall exposure of, say, 12 seconds but the 20-second step may be right for the sky, while a dark clump of trees in the middle distance needs only 8 seconds. To get the tonal balance right you would give a 20-second exposure to the print but after 8 seconds shade the trees and after 12 seconds shade all the land, leaving the sky to receive the full 20-second exposure.

With practice, you will soon develop your own style for shading and burning-in whether by dodging tools or simply with your hand. Local colour correction, however, will be a refinement that is needed only occasionally. Other printing controls—vignetting, flashing and correcting verticals—are explained next.

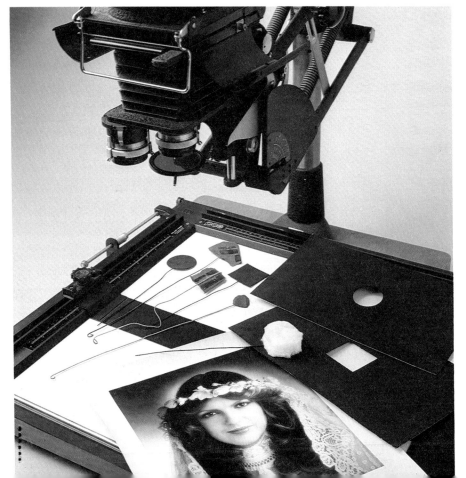

◀ A set of simple dodging tools can be easily made in an hour from readily-available materials. Don't use coat-hanger wire because it is too thick. Attach the pieces of card to the wire handles with staples, glue or adhesive tape.

Although shading, dodging and burning-in are used more frequently to improve prints, there are other equally useful manipulations such as correcting verticals, flashing and vignetting. And sooner or later you will find that a superb architectural shot has disturbing verticals which need to be made parallel, or a fairly ordinary photograph would be more appealing if vignetted. Flashing, however, applies only to black-and-white prints and is a rarely used technique.

Flashing

An otherwise unprintable negative which has little detail in the shadows and extremely dense highlights, which normally print to an unrelieved white, may be salvaged by this technique.

Flashing, as its name implies, consists of giving a very brief exposure to the printing paper with no negative in the enlarger before giving the normal exposure to the negative.

What happens is that flashing gives a very light exposure all over the paper which produces a slight tone in the highlights but has little effect in mid-tone and shadow areas.

The easiest way to give a flash exposure is to place a neutral density filter

(obtainable from your photographic supplier) of 2.0 density in the enlarger negative carrier instead of the negative and give the same exposure as for the negative. A 2.0 density filter transmits only 1/100 of the light falling on it, so if the exposure time is 10 seconds, the paper receives a flash exposure equivalent to 1/10 second.

▲ White highlights spoil this print. So flashing was tried. The paper was exposed normally, then given a second exposure to white light from a greatly dimmed 15 watt bulb for 2 seconds.

▼ This is the improved result.

BURNING-IN

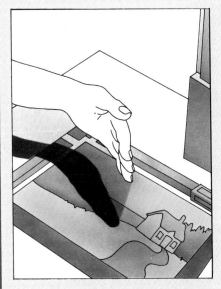

▲ Burn-in large areas, such as the sky by giving that part of the print increased exposure. Hold your hand or a piece of card over the image so it shades the lower half of the print. Burn-in smaller areas by cupping your hand or use a card with a hole in it.

▲ BEFORE
A dramatic photograph taken against a cloudy background. But the print, given an overall exposure of 10 seconds at f8, has a blank sky.
▼ AFTER
The solution is to burn-in the clouds by giving that part of

the print more exposure—an extra 15 seconds in this example, but use your test strip to assess the right amount. You can use your hand or a piece of card (black side facing down) to keep the light from the lower half of the print while you burn-in the sky.

SHADING

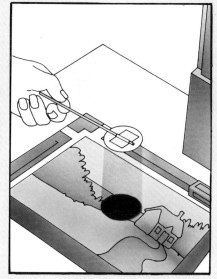

▲ To reduce or hold back the exposure for a small area, use a piece of card attached to stiff wire to shade the area during part of the exposure. But do not forget to keep the dodging tool moving to prevent hard edges from forming. The shaded area will be held back and therefore appear lighter in the print.

▲ **BEFORE**
This print was given a single 30-second exposure which was suitable for the boy and the exterior of the building, but too much for the interior which has lost its detail.

▼ **AFTER**
A small dodging tool was used to hold-back (shade) the interior so it received just

enough exposure (only 10 seconds) to reveal the blacksmith while the rest of the print received the full 30-second exposure. The photographer kept the dodger moving so no hard edges formed.

Correcting verticals

When you take a picture of a tall building you sometimes have to tilt the camera up to get the top of the building in the frame. This produces converging verticals which can ruin the photograph.

You can correct this distortion when you make the print by tilting the masking frame on the enlarger baseboard—but make sure that it can't move easily otherwise you may get a blurred print. Because one part of the image is now further from the enlarger (it should be the top of the building), it is enlarged progressively more than the rest so restoring the verticals.

On some enlargers you can tilt the negative carrier, which gives the same result. But the best solution is to tilt both the negative carrier and the masking frame in opposite directions,

because this lessens the angle to which each is tilted.

One part of the negative is enlarged more than another, so the image can only be brought into sharp focus over the whole area by stopping the lens down considerably. However, a few of the more advanced enlargers available also allow the lens panel to be tilted and when correctly adjusted the whole image can be made sharp even at full aperture.

When the masking frame is tilted, the part nearest to the enlarger lens will receive more exposure than the rest, so you must progressively burn-in the rest of the print slightly to avoid a gradual lightening in tone.

▼ **Inset shows how the verticals were converging before correction, as seen in the larger print.**

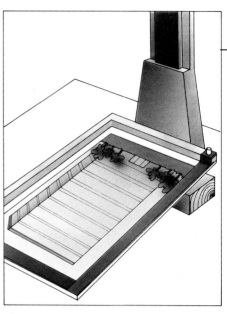

▲ **To correct verticals tilt the masking frame, supporting it on a block of wood or books.**

Vignetting

A step further on from burning-in is vignetting where only the central part of the paper is exposed to produce an image which gradually goes to white at the edges of the paper. To produce this result all you need is a piece of card with a fairly large oval shape cut in it. You then hold this in the same position as a normal dodger so that it casts a shadow over all but the central area of the paper.

▲ Vignettes normally refer to images where the edges fade off into white. However, they can be made with black borders instead. Expose the full sheet normally, then use an oval dodger to hold back the image while you fog the surrounding paper.

▶ Vignetting removes distracting surroundings and, when followed by sepia toning, is an effective way to turn records of family events into something rather special.

Making big black-and-white prints

There is an extra-special thrill about making your first really big print, perhaps one as large as 16 x 20in (40.6 x 50.8cm), but to obtain the quality you see in exhibitions you must take special care. In the first place, since the exposure needed is inevitably much longer than usual, the paper is out of the packet for a considerable time so the darkroom must be checked very carefully for light leaks, the enlarger head must not scatter any stray light and the safelight must not give even a trace of fog during the exposure. Any of these things, which may not affect a normal-sized print, can produce a greying of the highlights in a big enlargement and time spent looking for these causes of trouble is never wasted.

Adapting the enlarger

If your enlarger has a tall column it may be possible to make the print directly on the baseboard. This keeps the effect of vibration to a minimum since, if there is any movement, the head and the baseboard move as one unit. However, it may be necessary to turn the head or column round so that instead of projecting on to the baseboard the image is projected on to the floor, thus increasing the distance between the enlarger head and the paper. In this case it is essential to place a very heavy weight on the baseboard to counter-balance the weight of the head—a large pile of books can be used. Some enlargers have heads that can be swivelled to project horizontally so that the paper can be pinned to the wall or a door.

The lens: a standard focal length (50mm in the case of 35mm or 80mm with 2¼ x 2¼in—6 x 6cm) is needed to give sharp detail in the corners, though if only a small section of the negative is being printed it may be possible to use a shorter than normal focal length with the advantage that less distance is needed between the enlarger head and the paper.

● If you have a top-quality lens it can be closed down one stop for the exposure; inexpensive lenses usually have to be closed down two stops to obtain good corner definition. If the diaphragm is closed more than this the exposure will become too long.

● When you come to make the exposure, avoid using the switch on the baseboard if one is fitted since it may cause vibration. Instead, hold a sheet of card under the lens, turn on the enlarger and then remove the card.

Focusing: this is best done with the aid

When making big prints the focusing controls are often difficult to reach. The height of the Paterson Major Focus Finder helps to overcome this problem.

of a large focus finder. If an ordinary one is used you may find it hard to view the image and reach the focusing mechanism at the same time. However, specially tall ones are available which eliminate stretching.

The paper

Printing paper with a glossy surface gives maximum detail in the print but it also shows up any grain, dust or scratches and unless you are very experienced it may prove difficult to spot and retouch. Generally speaking a 'semi-matt' or 'smooth lustre' surface is more easily handled and does not show many reflections when the print is on display. Large packets of paper are expensive and if you have several negatives of varying contrast to print you may find the cost of having soft, normal and hard grades too high. Consequently there is a lot to be said for using a variable contrast paper such as 'Multigrade' because a very wide range of grades can be obtained from just one packet simply by varying the filter in the enlarging head, though against this must be balanced the cost of the set of filters.

Holding the paper: if you are making a normal-sized print you probably use a printing frame, but a frame to hold very large sheets of paper is expensive and

only justifies the cost if a large number of big prints is made. Instead many people use a sheet of heavy white card, marked with the size of the print they are making, for composing and focusing. The paper is fixed to this by means of double-sided self-adhesive tape or else with pins, though these will leave white marks at the corners that will have to be trimmed off when the print is dry.

Making a test strip

If you do not have an enlarging exposure meter a test strip is essential, and this will probably be larger than normal; it should cover an area of more or less equal density, the skin tones on a face, for instance, being easy to judge. Having determined the right contrast and exposure from the test strip, a full-sized print can now be made.

The processing dishes

A handyman may be tempted to make dishes large enough to take big prints from wood and hardboard lined with plastic or painted with waterproof paint. This is rarely worth while since they do not have a long life and cost almost as much as dishes made for the purpose. Although 16 x 20in (40.6 x 50.8cm) size plastic dishes are quite expensive, they are strong, chemical-proof and easily cleaned. Stainless steel trays are too expensive for amateur use while enamelled steel ones can chip or crack unless carefully handled.

Of course such dishes have other uses. They will serve as a water bath to stabilize the temperature of processing tanks or dishes. This is particularly applicable to colour where the higher processing temperatures are more likely to vary. They are also useful containers in which to wash your prints, so long as you ensure that there is good water circulation.

Processing the print

The normal processing chemicals—developer, stop bath and fixer—are used but a short development should be

▶ To make a big enlargement from a section of a negative, it is often necessary to turn the enlarger head and column round and project the image on to the floor. When doing this, make sure that the weight used to counterbalance the enlarger head is heavy enough to keep it securely positioned and free of vibration while you are working.

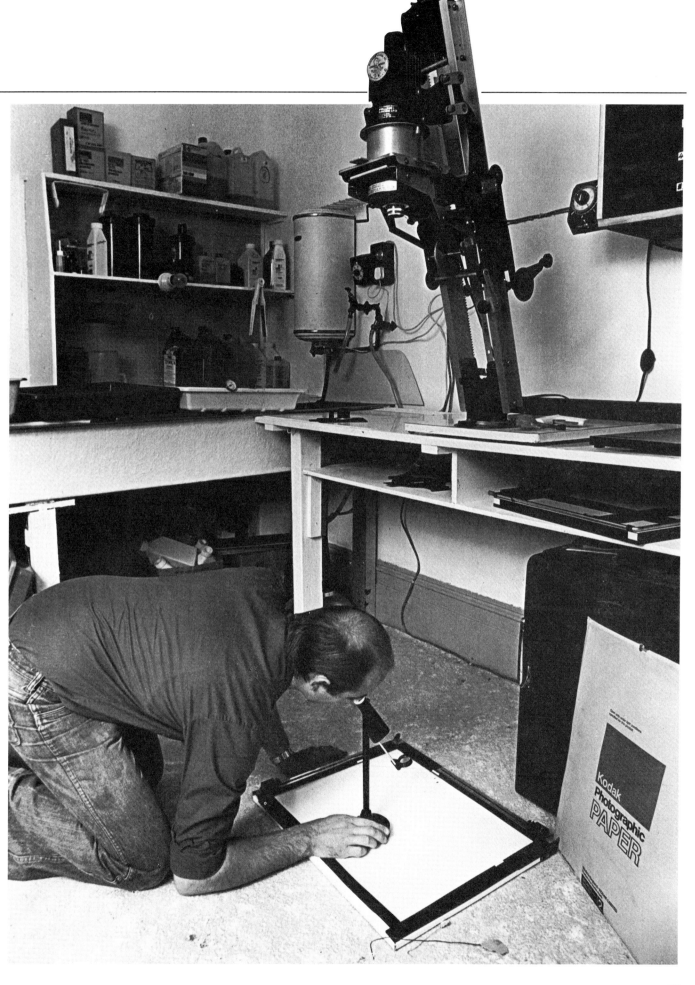

avoided since it may give an uneven result; 2-2½ minutes at 68°F (20°C) is about right. Don't skimp on the amount of chemicals used—a minimum depth of ½in (12mm) is needed.

Having slid the paper into the developer the dish must be rocked in both directions immediately so that the paper surface is covered as quickly and as evenly as possible. Continue rocking throughout the whole of the development and then transfer the print to the stop bath. It is not easy to handle very large prints with tongs and instead the fingers may have to be used. If you think that you may be allergic to chemicals wear plastic or rubber gloves.

After the usual times in the stop bath and fixer, and having made sure that the print is completely below the surface in both cases, the print must be washed thoroughly and this may call for the use of a bath. In theory you could use one of the processing dishes but they will probably be in use for other prints. Whatever method you use, the wash water must be changed constantly, the washing time being at least half an hour if ordinary fibre-based materials are used or about five minutes in the case of the modern resin-coated papers.

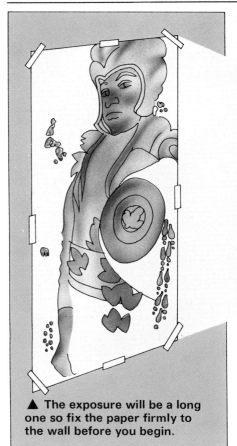

▲ The exposure will be a long one so fix the paper firmly to the wall before you begin.

▼ **If you project the negative on to a wall it is essential to check that the enlarger head is perfectly horizontal and the negative carrier is parallel to the wall. If they are not the image will be distorted.**

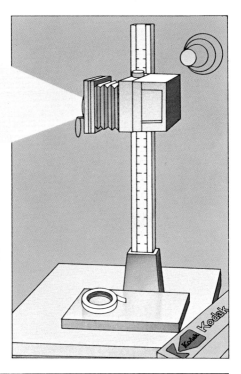

▼ **Processing giant prints is best done in long narrow dishes. Unroll and re-roll the print so that the processing solutions flow across the emulsion surface. The normal processing times for sheets of paper are used.**

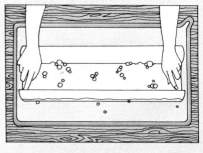

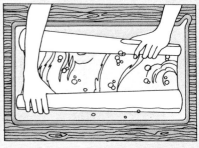

Giant enlargements

Prints larger than 16 x 20in (40.6 x 50.8cm), are not easy to do at home. However, the well-organized club with access to a darkroom may have the space necessary. They will also have the money to invest in the large rolls of paper used. It follows that if you do attempt to produce prints measured in feet or metres rather than inches or centimetres a different method of working must be adopted.

The first step is to acquire an enlarger with a head that can be turned to a horizontal position. The image is projected on to a wall, preferably one covered in a material into which drawing pins can be stuck. Once you have aligned the image, checked that it is square and the size you require, mark the outline with chalk or stick drawing pins in at appropriate points.

The developer, stop bath and fixer can most economically be laid out in narrow pans or troughs that are wider than the roll of paper.

The test strip should be a large one if it is to be useful. Processing it is good practice for the full-sized print. Having been stored in a roll, the strip will have a tendency to roll up. The curled strip is placed in the developer and rolled and re-rolled, making sure that the leading edge is pushed into the solution and that the developer flows over the emulsion surface. Continue to roll and re-roll the test strip for the normal development time. Processing in the stop bath and fixer follows the same procedure. Washing of large prints is best done in a bathtub.

A large draughtsman's T-square and a sharp knife are the best equipment to cut the paper for the full-sized print from the roll of paper. To avoid damaging the paper, handle the T-square with care. Bruise marks may not become obvious until after you have finished processing and have wasted a lot of time and paper. The print follows the same processing procedures as the test strip. To dry it a line is fixed above the bath and the print hung from it. Weights must be attached to prevent the print from curling.

Print finishing

After washing, as much water as possible should be removed from the print surface by means of a soft viscose sponge or a large rubber-bladed print squeegee. The print is then hung in a current of warm air by a clip at one corner or else laid face down on a sheet of photographic blotting paper. If you make a lot of large prints it may be worth making a wooden frame covered with muslin on which to lay the prints. Trimming large prints requires a different technique to the trimming of smaller ones. The most practical and economical approach is to use a metal-sided ruler that is longer than the longest side to be cut, and a very sharp scalpel or craft knife. The print should be laid flat on a dry clean surface. Check that the ruler is clean as well. Line up the ruler so that it covers part of the image and hold it firmly in place. Cutting on the 'outside' edge of the ruler ensures that, should your hand slip, no damage to the image results. Large prints made on ordinary paper inevitably curl when dry and should be mounted if intended for display. Resin-coated paper lies flat but should still be mounted if over 11 x 14in (30.5 x 40.6cm) in size so that the print can be handled easily.

▼ ▶ **When making prints as big as 30 x 40in (75 x 100cm) the image grain will be very noticeable. Marks on the negative will also be magnified. Check the negative carefully before starting to avoid a lot of retouching later.**

Black-and-white printing from colour originals

You may sometimes find that you want to make black-and-white prints from colour negatives or slides. For instance, you may find it helpful to make black-and-white proof enlargements from colour negatives to judge such things as expression or pose before going to the expense of making colour prints. Also picture editors on newspapers and some magazines prefer black-and-white prints unless they are producing a special colour supplement. If you have done your own black-and-white enlarging you will have almost all the equipment that you need. You can use an ordinary enlarger and the same trays and solutions you would use for black-and-white prints. For prints from slides, however, you will first need to make a black-and-white negative. You will then use this to produce a black-and-white print in the normal way.

Prints from colour negatives

Some people use conventional paper for making black-and-white prints from colour negatives but they soon find that their results suffer from tonal distortions. One of the reasons is that such papers are sensitive only to blue light so that they don't respond to green and red. The result is that red objects print too dark while blue areas print too light. For example, lips and pink complexions appear dark while blue skies with white clouds reproduce with little detail.

Grain size

Another unfortunate side-effect when working from colour negatives is an increase in the apparent size of the grain. For example, prints from an extremely fine grain colour film such as Kodacolor II 100 ASA may appear more grainy than prints from similar size negatives taken on a high speed black-and-white film. This arises because the yellow dye granules in the colour negative are quite large and, because yellow is complementary to blue, the blue sensitive paper records them as quite a bit darker than the eye sees them. Thus attention is drawn to them and they become very obvious to the eye.

The answer is to use a panchromatic paper such as Kodak Panalure II RC paper. With this paper you can produce a print which looks very like one from a negative taken on normal panchromatic film. All the colours are reproduced in their appropriate shades of grey.

You handle this paper in the same way as you handle colour paper, working with a colour safelight or in complete darkness. Don't use safelights designed

◀ Most people use colour negative film these days. However that doesn't mean you have to do without black-and-white prints. When you have a portrait like this that you may want to send to relatives it is far cheaper to produce the copies in black-and-white.

Below left: Panalure paper is sensitive to all colours and layers of the film and gives a smooth even result which is needed on this formal portrait.

Below: printing a colour negative on bromide paper gives a grainy result. The paper responds mainly to blue light and the yellow dye layer in the film has a very coarse grain structure which the paper records.

▶ Sometimes the exaggeration of grain produced by bromide paper can be used to good effect. In an informal portrait it can add to the atmosphere. Here *Tim Cook* used it to soften the outlines of the image. By making a light print and sepia toning it he further enhanced the effect.

for conventional black-and-white papers or the paper will be fogged.

You don't need colour printing filters in your enlarger when you expose Panalure paper. Just produce your enlargement in the same way you would with black-and-white negatives, making a test series of exposures first to get the correct exposure for your

own conditions. The series should range from about 7 seconds to 30 seconds at f8 so that you have a good selection to choose from. Panalure paper can be processed in most general purpose black-and-white print developers and fixing solutions.

Unlike conventional papers, it's best not to develop Panalure papers by inspection. If you do so you will find the safelight illumination so low that you will have difficulty estimating when the density is right. Instead, use the strictly controlled time and temperature method of development that you would use for films or colour paper. At 68°F (20°C) the recommended development time is 1½ minutes. If you follow this procedure not only will your results be more satisfactory but image tones will remain constant from one print to the next.

Using filters

For greater effect you can use filters just as you would on your camera lens and the same rules apply: to darken a colour use a filter of a complementary colour; to lighten a colour use a filter of a similar colour. For example, you can darken blue skies by using a deep yellow filter on the enlarger. The same filter will lighten the golden colour of wheat fields, although for a more dramatic effect you may want to use a red filter.

When you've decided what you want to do just tape the appropriate filter on to the front of the enlarger lens. As with all filters you will need to increase exposure to compensate for the light they absorb. As a guide, use the same filter factor as you would for a panchromatic film in tungsten lighting. For example, a deep yellow filter has a

factor of about 2x and a red filter has a factor of about 5x under these conditions. However, to be really sure make a test strip with the filter in position.

Prints from colour slides

Before you can make a print from a slide you need to produce a black-and-white negative. There are several ways of doing this, most of them using equipment you already have.

Using a projector: the easiest method is to use a medium speed panchromatic film such as Kodak Plus-X Pan film or Ilford FP4 in a 35mm camera. Use a slide projector to throw your transparency on to a smooth screen, a matt white wall or a sheet of white paper. Don't use a beaded screen or a rough-surfaced material otherwise you may pick up the texture in your photograph and the result will look like grain in the finished print.

Position your camera as close as you can to the projector lens-to-screen axis without interfering with the image. Determine the exposure by taking a meter reading off the screen from the camera position and to be really sure of getting a good negative, bracketing your exposures. Develop the film as you would normally.

This technique can produce good quality negatives but only if you make every effort to reduce light flare. Use a clean, good quality lens on the projector, a dark surround to the projected image area and ban smoking while you are at work.

Using a slide copier: for better quality results use one of the many slide copying devices on the market. Again, use a medium speed panchromatic film and estimate exposure as directed in the duplicator instructions.

Some copiers have a method of reducing contrast. You will find this useful for all but low contrast slides. Try a few tests with and without contrast reduction. Using your normal processing conditions you will soon discover the best technique to adopt for your own slides.

Using your enlarger: both methods just described are capable of giving good quality negatives, but for the best quality you should use an enlarger. The technique is not the easiest to use but it does allow you more control over the final quality than other methods. Unfortunately some 35mm enlargers will not give small enough images on the printing frame. Unless the normal 50mm lens can be replaced with a

75mm, enlargers with this limitation cannot be used for this technique.

Place your slide in the enlarger negative carrier and compose the image on the printing frame. If the frame surface is white make sure that it is covered with black paper during exposure to prevent light reflecting from it. Ensure that the image area is no bigger than the largest negative accepted by your carrier. Make sure that your darkroom is really dark and that your enlarger is light-tight. If you do have to light-proof it take care that it doesn't overheat the enlarger head while you are using it.

Use a medium speed panchromatic sheet film such as Kodak Plus-X Pan film or Ilford FP4 cut down to size. Make a test series to determine the correct exposure, stopping down the lens as far as it will go and using very short exposures starting at 1 second.

Most slides are high contrast subjects so you may need to reduce contrast. You can adjust the development time to do this. A reduction of 25-30% should be sufficient.

Once you have your black-and-white negative you can use it like any other black-and-white negative. You can make prints on any of the range of conventional black-and-white papers.

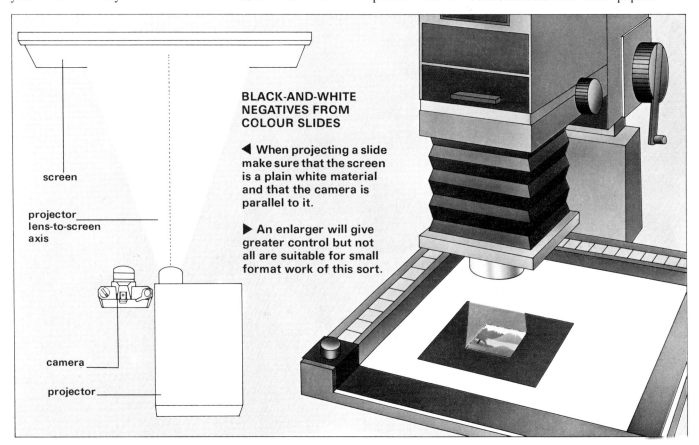

screen

projector
lens-to-screen
axis

camera

projector

BLACK-AND-WHITE NEGATIVES FROM COLOUR SLIDES

◀ When projecting a slide make sure that the screen is a plain white material and that the camera is parallel to it.

▶ An enlarger will give greater control but not all are suitable for small format work of this sort.

▲ A vivid subject in colour can prove difficult to transfer to black-and-white on occasions, particularly when red and green are involved.

▲ Enlarging the slide directly on to panchromatic film produces very little difference between the flower and the background foliage.

▲ A deep red filter taped to the lens of the enlarger lightens all the red in the image and makes the green darker to give the flower prominence.

▲ Most slides have a greater contrast range than prints. To retain both highlights and shadow detail in the print, development will often need to be altered when using an enlarger.

1 Given a standard development time a negative can be quite contrasty. Detail in the face and background will be lost unless special care is taken at the printing stage.

2 Reducing development by 25% is enough to alter the negative contrast range sufficiently for it to be printed on your usual grade of paper.

Colour toning

Having tried sepia toning, you are probably ready to attempt something more adventurous and colour toning is an obvious progression. The techniques are similar and you can buy kits that include sepia as well as other colours. The range of colours is rich—purple, green, yellow, red and blue, and variations of these effects by applying one colour over another. Berg, Colorvir and Pebeo all produce kits for this work.

There are two main types of toner —metal toners and colour developers. But whichever product you use, always follow the manufacturer's directions carefully if you want good results.

Metal toners

These toners convert the silver image into either a coloured metal compound or a compound containing silver and a coloured metal. The images produced, though often vivid in colour, are relatively impermanent. Their use is somewhat restricted and in most cases the colour developer method produces more permanent and more attractive results.

The actual colour formed depends on the metal compound used. Examples are iron (as potassium ferricyanide); which yields blue; lead acetate—yellow; cobalt chloride—green; copper sulphate—red. Again, you may either prepare your own solutions from a formula or you can buy pre-mixed kits of chemicals. It is wise to experiment with a spare print before working on a prized picture.

Most of these metal toners are one-bath processes, but some consist of two baths; the first bath is a bleach and the second a toner. After toning, RC prints should be washed for about 5 minutes and ordinary prints for 30 minutes. Prints which have previously been sepia toned may produce pleasing colours when metal toned. For instance, red to orange tones are produced when sepia-toned prints are further toned with an iron (blue) toner.

◄ You can make two-tone prints. Here bleach for the sepia process was applied with a brush to the beach, painting it carefully along the edge of the sea. The whole print was then washed and placed in sepia toner— which doesn't affect the sea area. Finally blue toner was applied to the sea by brush. Painting on toner can lead to streaking. It is normally better to tone in a dish and agitate continuously. But you must use Strip Mask to protect the areas of the print which are not to be toned by that particular colour.

▲ The choice of colour is highly personal and as you can see from these examples by no means an obvious choice. Blue is often recommended for subjects where there is a lot of water, or snow or moonlight. By selecting a more unusual colour, however, the mood of a picture can be changed markedly. Look for images which are strong yet simple and with a full range of tones.
With all toning, the black and white print should be clean and pre-wet by soaking in water for 2-5 minutes. It is then drained and toned, according to the method.

◀ Fishing platforms at the edge of the sea in France have become a work of art through a combination of reticulation and colour toning. For reticulation the film was loaded on to the spiral and plunged alternately into very hot and icy water. The film is then developed normally. (You could also use a reticulation screen when making the print.) Using the Colorvir system the print was given 10 min. in the solarizer yellow bath, 12 min. in the red J bath (followed by treatment in weak acetic acid to soften the red) and finally put into polychromie blue.

▼ Colour toning can also be combined with a chemical solarizing solution in the Colorvir system. The print should be soaked as usual in water for up to 5 minutes before placing it in the first process bath. This green solarized print of a Paris street scene went through a combined yellow toner and solarization bath and finally it was put into a blue toner.

Colour developers

This method gives the widest range of possible colours and consists of three basic steps: rehalogenating bleach which converts the black metallic silver to silver bromide; colour development which gives a dye image and regenerates the original silver image; silver-removing bleach which leaves only the dye image. The print is washed between each of these steps and sometimes the silver-removing bleach is replaced by a separate rehalogenating bleach followed by a wash and then a fixing bath. The final wash should again be 5 minutes for RC prints.

In the colour developer step, the dye produced depends on the colour former (coupler) present—in fact, a range of colours can be obtained by varying the proportions of these colour formers. Experiment on a spare print or cut one $20 \cdot 3 \times 25 \cdot 4$cm print into four and vary the proportions of the colour formers to achieve the colour you want. It is also possible to shorten the time for silver-removing bleach to leave some black metallic silver in the print to give darker shadow areas.

It is not practical to mix your own chemicals and it is far simpler to buy one of the readily available kits. The colour developer does not keep very well once mixed and should therefore be prepared just before use.

Toning of black and white prints can be used to produce a wide range of coloured images but it is worth making a few experiments before you tone one of your fine quality prints. Remember to be meticulously clean in your work. Once you have mastered the basic techniques you can move on to 'mixed' or partial toning, using a small brush to apply the toner or bleach to the desired areas. Pre-soak the print and use an upturned developing dish placed over the sink as a work surface. Use water from a running tap to stop the bleach.

There are many Colorvir combinations. Top left: blue toning, yellow toning, red dyeing. Top right: solarization, violet dye, red dye. Bottom left: yellow toning plus freezing the grey solution, then polychromie blue. Bottom right: yellow toning plus freezing the grey, then red and blue polychromie dyes mixed. Use prints made on Kenthene or other RC papers.

Black-and-white emergency measures

No matter how well you have mastered the art of developing your black-and-white films, there is always a moment of suspense as you draw the film from the reel. The more important the subject matter on the films, the greater the pulse rate. In most cases the film will reveal a dozen or so well exposed frames. Each negative image will contain a range of densities from light to dark and all will be well.

Occasionally, however, things go wrong such as a slip up when setting the film speed, or a misreading of the developer temperature or processing time. Such mistakes can result in negatives with too dense an image or images that are far too thin. In extreme cases they will be difficult to print and the cost will be high in terms of time and printing paper.

Often you can discard faulty negatives and put the whole thing down to experience. Sometimes, however, the images may be too important—like a wedding or the birth of your child, for example—to be dismissed so casually. In these cases you will want to salvage as much detail as possible.

The most appropriate line of attack depends on whether the negatives have been over-exposed and/or over-developed, in which case you may need to use reduction, or whether they have been under-exposed and/or under-developed, in which case you will perhaps need to use intensification. These are both chemical treatments; reduction, as its name implies, acts on the silver and by dissolving some of it decreases the density. Intensification does the reverse—it either increases the density of the image by adding another metal to the silver image or it stains the image, making it less transparent to light. Most intensifiers unfortunately increase the grain.

It must be stressed that these are emergency measures and as such cannot be expected to turn the negative into A1 quality.

Materials

The most widely used intensifiers and reducers are available in the form of prepared chemicals from some of the large photographic retailers and mail order suppliers. Before buying a preparation, it is worth checking, either with the supplier or the manufacturer, that the treatment you select will produce the desired effect. If you are in a shop ask to see the instructions. You should always read the instructions

You will need
1 Tubes of powdered reducer
2 Solutions of reducer and intensifier
3 Measuring cylinders
4 Plastic gloves
5 White processing dish
6 Fine painting brushes
7 Cotton wool
8 Cotton buds
9 Mixing palette
10 Scissors

Step-by-step to intensifying the negative

1 WASHING THE NEGATIVE
Begin the process by thoroughly rewashing the negative. This removes any traces of fixer. It also makes the gelatin swell. Dry gelatin is very absorbent and if film is placed in the solution of intensifier without washing it will absorb too much.

2 BLEACHING
Once the negative is washed immerse it in the intensifier solution.
Agitate continuously until the black silver image is completely bleached to a pale buff colour. Take care when doing this as the solution is corrosive and will damage clothing.

3 THE SECOND WASH
Wash the negative thoroughly for about five minutes until the overflow is clear and colourless.

carefully before you begin work on your negatives.

You will need a small, white, plastic container (not one used for food—keep it exclusively for photographic work) or a small developing dish in which to process the negative, and some measures for making up your solutions.

Finally, when handling photographic chemicals it is always advisable to avoid contact with the skin. Thin plastic gloves, which are available from most drugstores or chemists, protect the hands and are ideal for tackling the delicate manoeuvres necessary when handling small pieces of film and working on individual areas of photographic prints.

Rescuing faulty negatives

In some cases you may be able to compensate for the lack of quality in the negative by printing on a suitable grade of paper, but if this doesn't work you will need to use chemical treatment. If you have to resort to this always remember to rewash the negative to be treated before you begin.

Under-developed negatives look thin and lifeless because they lack contrast though they may contain plenty of

information in both highlights and shadows. If the effects are not too marked, you may be able to produce a passable print by using a hard grade of paper. But in extreme cases you will need to resort to intensification.

Intensifiers increase the density of the image in proportion to the existing density so highlights are intensified more than shadows, which increases the contrast of the negative. A widely used metal intensifier is a chromium preparation in which the proportions of the working solution can be varied according to the degree of intensification required.

Leave the negative in the working solution until it has been bleached to a yellow-buff colour and then rinse it

thoroughly in water. Finally, the negative is redeveloped in an ordinary print developer.

Under-exposed negatives show details in the highlights but contain little or no detail in the shadows, and in extreme cases of under-exposure these areas are clear film. This type of negative is very difficult to print and is not greatly improved by intensification because nothing can be deposited where there is no image. If you are determined to rescue this negative, of those intensifiers readily available, chromium will give the best results.

Over-developed negatives are dense and contrasty. They contain plenty of information in the shadow areas, but detail in the highlight areas is clogged

▲ A typically under-developed negative lacks contrast but does possess a little shadow detail. The print looks very dull and lifeless. It is difficult to print on harder grades of paper and must be intensified.

▲ The intensified negative lacks the fineness of definition and smooth contrast range of a properly developed negative. However it will print to give an acceptable result and thus overcome an often difficult situation.

4. REDEVELOPMENT
Redevelop the negative in any standard print developer until the buff image has gone completely black. This usually takes 2-3 minutes at 68°F (20°C). Wash for a minute and then refix in a fixing solution containing hardener. Finally wash again and dry.

in an excess of silver. A slightly over-developed negative can sometimes be printed on a softer grade of paper. Considerable over-development requires reduction of the negative and for this you need a super-proportional reducer which will remove silver in proportion to that which is already there, taking more from the highlight areas than the shadows and thus reducing contrast. Ammonium persulphate will do this but can only be made up from high quality chemicals and has to be used immediately.

Over-exposed negatives are dense and lack contrast. They contain all the details of the subject buried in too much silver. If this effect is too extreme to be remedied by printing on a harder grade of paper you will need to resort to reduction. Here single bath Farmer's reducer, such as Tetenal reducer, is used. (There is also a potassium per-manganate reducer.) These are known as proportional reducers because they tend to reduce in proportion to the amount of silver already there. However, in practice there is less density in those areas derived from the shadows of the original subject and so reduction is noticeable in those areas first.

The actual treatment is easy enough. You dilute the reducer as directed and immerse the washed negative until there has been sufficient decrease in density. As you are checking this visually it is best to use a white tray or container. When reduction has gone far enough just remove the negative and wash it thoroughly. As the diluted reducer becomes useless after about 15 minutes it is best to make up a small quantity for each treatment.

Rescuing prints
There should be little need for emer-gency measures in black-and-white printing if you follow the procedure of making test strips. In the case of big enlargements, if you do slip up, you may want to try and rescue the print. For example, if the print is over-exposed it is possible to lighten it by immersing the print for 5 to 10 seconds in a weak solution of Farmer's reducer

▶ Always work slowly when bleaching parts of a print. Remember to wash it every minute to prevent staining.

▼ Sometimes it is not possible to take a photograph in the way you would like. Here background detail distracts from the subject. To remove it work gradually in from the edge towards the subject, bleaching the print section by section. Never be tempted by short cuts. One mistake can mean that you have to start all over again.

— use a one bath working solution and dilute it by one part of solution to five parts of water.

Local reduction of prints to lighten small areas—for example, around the eyes in a portrait—can also be carried out with a weak solution of Farmer's reducer applied with a brush or a small swab of cotton or Q-tips (cotton buds). You treat the print after it has been fixed and washed but while it is still damp. The solution acts quite rapidly so watch it carefully. Work near a tap so that you can rinse the print every minute. This will avert any staining. After treatment, wash and dry the print in the usual way.

Local intensification of prints is not possible. However, if as you develop the print, you can see that there is too little detail appearing in parts of the image, you can help things along if you are quick. To do this you can increase the action of the developer in a particular area by the local application of heat: simply rub the area with the ball of your finger while the print is in the developer. You can also apply concentrated developer on a swab of cotton to obtain a small increase in local density and contrast. The paper then needs to be rinsed, fixed and washed in the normal way. Be wary of this procedure—over-zealous action can lead to print staining.

Special precautions

It is worth taking the following precautions to be certain of the best chance of successfully treating your negatives.

● The negative image must be correctly fixed.

● Make a really good print from the faulty negative before treatment—just in case the negative gets damaged.

● Do a trial run first with an old unwanted negative to test the method.

● Wash the negative thoroughly before you start working on it. This ensures that the film gelatine has swollen evenly and that disproportionate acceptance of the chemicals does not occur because the film is in its dry, highly absorbent state.

● Treat only one negative image at a time.

● Hold the negative by the edges only —wet negatives are easily scratched.

● While the negatives are being treated for reduction or intensification agitate continuously.

● Some of these chemicals are very poisonous and should be locked away when not in use.

Retouching

A small amount of simple retouching can often transform a rather unattractive spotty print into something you can be proud of. Most of your retouching work will be done on prints (black-and-white and colour), as negatives and transparencies are very difficult to work on.

Basic equipment

For basic print retouching you need: a good quality brush (around 00 size), which you can buy from an art materials shop; retouching dyes—obtainable from your photographic suppliers; absorbent material such as blotting paper or paper tissues; a small hobby knife—the sort which comes with detachable, sharp blades (the rounded blades are best); a small vessel to hold water (such as a small jam jar); and a flat surface for mixing dyes (a saucer or painter's palette).

Most of these materials are available in ready-made retouching kits which can be bought from photographic suppliers. It is very important to look after your brushes and to ensure that the hairs do not become straggly. If your brush comes with a small plastic sheath, always make sure you replace it after use, as a damaged brush is of little use to anyone.

White spots on the print

Even if you are a meticulous worker and you take every precaution to avoid marks appearing on your prints, there are always a few dust specks which will show up as white spots on the print. Occasionally, a negative gets scratched and as a result you may have black spots and lines to remove on the print.

If you find that your prints have a large number of unwanted marks, you should check your enlarger and other equipment for dust. The main problems arise from dust in the negative carrier, especially when it has glass, and for this reason many photographers prefer glassless negative carriers. Unfortunately, the glassless carrier makes it more difficult to maintain a flat negative and therefore an overall sharp image. No one system is perfect; you should try both and see which you prefer.

The use of cans of compressed air, blower brushes and cleaning brushes (preferably of the antistatic type) helps to keep dust away from the negative and carrier.

The white spots, caused by small dust particles on the negative or carrier, are removed by adding small amounts of retouching dye. There are three types of dye; watercolour paints which are unsuitable for glossy prints because they leave surface marks, water-soluble powder dyes which again tend to leave surface marks on glossy prints and—best of all—photographic dyes which do not mar the print surface.

Select the dye colour which most closely matches the tone of your black-and-white prints; the image tone of black-and-white prints depends on the type of paper and varies from warm browns through neutrals, to blue-blacks. Before you begin, make sure that your work area is clean and that you have enough light and that it does not cause distracting reflections on the print surface; a gooseneck lamp placed to one side is ideal.

Make up a weak solution of dye and immerse your brush in it. Now remove most of the dye solution from the brush by gently stroking the brush tip on an absorbent material such as blotting paper or paper tissue, and work the tip of the brush to a point. Using the brush in a stippling manner, add dye to the white spots which are within areas of the same tone or darker than the dye mixture in the brush. It is important, however, that the brush is kept almost dry.

The idea is to gradually add dye to the white spots and build their density until it matches the surrounding area. It is best to work outwards from the centre of the area to be retouched. This building-up of dye prevents dark areas appearing near the edge of the retouched area.

Continue this stippling technique until all the spots within the lighter tones are camouflaged. Now increase the strength of your dye until a mid-tone is achieved. Using the same technique, retouch all the white spots within the mid-greys. Finally, increase the dye strength, possibly as undiluted dye, and retouch all the dark areas.

There are not quick ways to retouch a print; it simply requires patience, care and practice. It is obviously best to learn by practising on reject prints.

Black lines and spots

Black marks on a print are caused by white marks on the negative, and may result from scratches, dust in the camera, or dust in processing.

The first step is to remove the black spots by 'knifing', which is done by scraping the spots very carefully with a small hobby knife. Again, it is best to

remove the black spots very gradually, working down from black through a mid-tone to a white. Sometimes it is possible to scrape the darker area until it exactly matches the surrounding area, although in practice this may be difficult. Generally speaking, it is best to produce a tone lighter than the surrounding area. This light tone is then 'rebuilt' to the adjacent tone by the method described previously for filling in white spots.

Chemical reduction

Where easily-accessible areas of a print need to be partially or completely removed, as in the case of a distracting background, it is often best to use chemical reduction. This technique involves rewetting the print and carefully, with a Q-tip (cotton bud) or brush, applying a bleaching solution (such as Farmer's reducer or iodine bleach) to the necessary area. The strength of the bleach should be tested first on a reject print, before starting work on your best print.

This method works best on a part of a print where a gradual reduction is required over a fairly large area, or where small defects appear on an otherwise clear background. Chemical reduction is usually much quicker than conventional retouching techniques.

▲ **A well-lit surface is important for successful retouching. When applying the dye protect the lower part of the print with a clean tissue or piece of paper. Start with the lighter tones and build up the density gradually till it matches the surrounding tone. Test dye strength, first, on a plain piece of paper. Don't overload the brush, and spot the dye by stippling.**
Insets show how to hold the brush for stippling and how to control the blade in knifing out. Though a 00 brush gives more control, you may want to use a bigger brush.

How to make pictures that last

Photographs have always been taken for the same reason— to provide a permanent record of the passing moment. As the years go by these records grow in value and importance. Yet if the pictures do not last but fade away or change colour with the passing of time the whole exercise is self-defeating.

Pictures, including paintings, have always faded or changed. Many early photographs have deteriorated irretrievably, and the reason we think 19th-century processes were more permanent is that the only examples we see are those prints that have survived.

What precautions can be taken to prevent pictures deteriorating? Problems of preservation can be split into three sections: preservation of black-and-white prints, preservation of colour prints, and preservation of original negatives and slides. An additional distinction may also be made between preservation for ordinary purposes, the prints lasting, say, up to 20 years, and long-term or 'archival' storage of 100 years or even longer.

Black-and-white prints

The image on black-and-white prints is usually silver. This is a reactive metal which readily combines with gases in the air, which is why silver objects tarnish. Old prints often show a blackish sheen on the surface in places. This is silver sulphide and can be avoided by storing prints where fumes, especially those containing sulphur compounds, cannot reach them. If the image turns yellowish in patches or fades away this is usually caused by incorrect fixing or washing.

Fixing

It is very important to use fresh fixer for long-lasting prints.
● A good method is to have two fixer baths. The first does most of the work leaving the second, fresher bath as a safety measure to make sure that the fixed emulsion can be washed easily. After several prints have been fixed the second bath becomes the first and a new second bath is prepared. Give prints half the manufacturer's recom-

mended fixing time in the first bath, then transfer them to the second to complete fixation.
● Keep a record of the total volume of fixer used, and make sure that you don't try to fix more prints than the recommended capacity.
● Always allow prints sufficient time in the fixer and move them occasionally while fixing.
● Prints on resin-coated (RC) papers should not be fixed too long because liquid can start to soak in at the cut edges, making them impossible to wash properly. However, the edges can be trimmed off afterwards.

Washing

Washing must be done well. Fibre-based papers take half an hour or longer to wash. RC prints wash more swiftly— five minutes or so is usually ample.
● The water should not be too cold. When the temperature goes below 59°F (15°C) chemicals wash out more slowly— the ideal is 64.4°F to 75.2°F (18°C to 24°C).

Acid-free print storage box

Selenium toner

Gold toner

High speed fixer and washing aid

Fibre-based papers

To protect your prints, use a gold or selenium toner. Then keep them in acid-free storage boxes.

Ilford's Galerie system includes a Washaid which helps to remove fixer from fibre-based paper. Use a non-hardening fixer for thorough print washing with Washaid.

● Make sure fixer-laden water from the bottom of the washing container can drain away—there is no point in having fresh water flow in at the top and away again while prints sit in a stagnant pool below.

● Prints wash more easily if the fixer is not a hardening one, though this means care may be needed with delicate emulsions—for example, Ilford Multigrade—that can be damaged easily when wet. It is a good plan to make a test on a print occasionally to check that your washing procedure is efficient. Commercially available testing solutions are simple to use: you put a drop of the liquid on the print margin and see if it changes colour. One way to speed up washing is to use a 'hypo eliminator', but modern research does not recommend this. An idea which does work is the washing accelerator produced by Ilford for their Galerie paper-base materials. After a preliminary wash the print is soaked in this bath, which loosens the hold the fixer has on the fibres of the paper. The print is then washed again. This method will work with all papers of the older type, not just Galerie, and instead of the special chemical you can use a solution of sodium sulphite.

Toning for permanence

A good way of preserving the silver image in a print is to convert it into a more stable chemical compound. A slight change in image colour will also result. Turning the silver into silver sulphide (usually warm brown or sepia) or selenium sulphide (brown with hints of purple) is quite simple, and ready-made chemicals can be bought.

An excellent alternative is gold toner, but this is very expensive and tends to give a bluish tone suitable for snow scenes, seascapes and the like. The layer of inert gold formed does give the silver image of the print a high degree of protection.

Other processes such as carbon and platinum printing are too specialized for general use.

▶ **Superior negatives deserve to be made into superior prints. This picture by *Naru* was printed by Adrian Ensor on Ilford Galerie, which is designed to give long lasting prints when processed with special chemicals. Compared with other fibre-based papers, Galerie has a less brilliant base tint, a good tonal range with rich shadows, and slightly lower contrast for each grade. It suits negatives like this very well.**

Glossary

Words in *italics* appear as separate entries

A

Acclerator The chemical in a developer which speeds up development, usually an alkaline salt, such as sodium carbonate or borax.

Acid fixer A *fixer* which includes an acid, usually acetic acid.

Acutance A measurement of image sharpness which is dependent on the film emulsion and the developer. A laboratory test determines acutance from how rapidly image tones change between light and dark on going across a 'knife-edge'. Images of high actuance show high contrast across edges and appear sharper than images containing the same subject detail but low acutance. Special high acutance developers make images appear sharper but, unfortunately, images produced this way also appear grainier (show a peppery effect).

Agitation The technique of moving or stirring a solution to ensure even and consistent processing. The amount of development or other processing, (for example, fixing) that occurs depends partly on the degree of agitation. (However, time, temperature and chemical formulation are also important.)

Air bells Small bubbles of air which stick to the surface of the emulsion on films and printing papers, and stop the developer acting on the emulsion.

Alkali A substance with a Ph greater than 7. Alkalis are used in most developers and give the solution its 'slippery' feel. The stronger alkalis, such as sodium hydroxide (caustic soda), should be treated with care as they can cause serious burns.

ASA American Standards Association (former name of American National Standards Institute). The sensitivity (speed with which it reacts to light) of a film can be measured by the ASA standard or by other standards systems, such as DIN. The ASA film speed scale is arithmetical—a film of 200 ASA is twice as fast as a 100 ASA film and half the speed of a 400 ASA film

B

Base This is the support on which photographic materials are coated, and may be paper or a clear plastic (that is, film) such as cellulose triacetate. Base is also a general name for alkalis.

Baseboard The board on which an enlarger stands. An enlarger which does not have a baseboard big enough to contain large images can often be made to give large prints by swivelling the head round the column through 180°. The image is then projected on to, for example, the floor. With the enlarger head in this position, it is usually necessary to place a heavy weight on the baseboard to counterbalance the enlarger head.

Bleach A chemical bath that reacts with the black silver formed by the developer in one of two ways; either by converting it back to its original silver salts, or by dissolving the silver

completely. Most colour processes use the type of bleach which regenerates the original silver salts. Some black-and-white processes also use bleach, for example, sepia toning.

Bromide paper A popular type of black and white printing paper which gives a neutral or blue-black image colour. It gets its name because the emulsion used is silver bromide. The other main type of black and white paper is *chlorobromide* (for example, Bromesko, Ilfomar) which gives a warmer (browner) image colour.

Buffer Chemicals which help to maintain the pH (acidity or alkalinity) or chemical constitution of a solution, and so keep the solution activity constant. They are normally used in developer solutions to help give consistent processing. Examples are borax/boracic acid and sodium carbonate/sodium hydroxide.

Burning-in A printing technique where extra exposure is selectively given to parts of the image. In black-and-white printing burning-in darkens tones and modifies contrast (when using multicontrast papers); it is particularly useful for bringing out highlights. In colour printing, burning-in can modify both tone (density) and colour.

C

Characteristic curve The curved line on a graph which describes precisely how the photographic film or paper responds to light. These characteristic curves, sometimes called D log E curves, are used by photographic manufacturers for quality control.

Clearing bath The general name given to any processing step which is designed to remove or chemically neutralize any potentially harmful chemicals which are carried over by the film or paper.

Clearing time The time required in the fixer for the film to go from its initial milky appearance to a clear film. To ensure that fixing is complete it is normal to leave the film in the fixing bath for twice the clearing time. The clearing and fixing times depend on the formulation of the fixer, temperature, agitation, and the amount of use the solution has already had.

Compensating developer A developer which acts more vigorously on the less exposed area of the film and less actively on the more exposed areas. The net result is a reduction in negative contrast. At best, this compensating effect is only small, and is usually found when very dilute developers are used with a minimum of agitation.

Condenser A simple one-element lens which causes light to converge. These lenses are used in many enlargers to focus the light source on to the back of the enlarger lens. Their position or strength (focal length) may be varied according to the film size being enlarged.

Contact printing In this type of printing the film is held in contact with the printing paper and no lens is needed. Contact printing can be used for making prints from large films—4x5in

(10.2x12.7cm) and larger—or when contacts are required for inspection or records.

Continuous tone Any photographic material which is capable of producing a continuous range of tones from white to a maximum black. A continuous tone material shows subtlety of tone throughout its range, from rich shadows, through mid-greys, to delicate highlights.

Contrast The variation of image tones from the shadows of the scene, through its mid-tones, to the highlights. Contrast depends on the type of subject, scene brightness range, film, development and printing.

Contrast grade The number which indicates the contrast of photographic paper. The scale of numbers usually runs from 1 through to 5, with the most contrasty papers having the highest numbers. Negatives having a low contrast—referred to as soft negatives—are printed on to high—number paper grades such as 3 to 5, normal negatives should print best on grade 2, and high-contrast (hard) negatives on grades 0 and 1.

Contrast index A Kodak system designed to standardize negative printing characteristics. If a photographer develops all his films to the same CI, then he should obtain prints of similar quality on similar paper grades, provided that other factors, such as lighting and subject matter, are also standardized.

D

Darkroom A room which is sufficiently dark to enlarge and process photographic prints; and to handle, without fear of premature exposure (fogging), other photographic materials.

Density The ability of an area of a paper or film to absorb light. Areas of high density absorb a lot of light and appear black, whereas low-density areas absorb only a small amount of light and appear closer to white (theoretically having a density of zero). A density increase of 0.3 represents a doubling of light-stopping ability so a 1.3 density area absorbs twice as much light as another area of 1.0 density.

Density range The difference between the minimum density (D min) of a print or film and its maximum density (D max). Typical density ranges are 0-1.8 for black-and-white papers, 0-1.2 for black-and-white negatives.

Developer A solution which converts the latent image on exposed film or paper to a visible image. A black-and-white developer produces a black silver image, while a colour developer generates both a black silver image (removed in later steps) and a coloured image consisting of three dyes (yellow, magenta and cyan).

Developing by inspection This technique, whereby the paper or film is viewed periodically under a suitable safelight during processing, allows development to be terminated at exactly the desire time. Development by inspection is only practical for papers and some slower films.

Developing tank A container in which film or paper is developed. The film is loaded on a spiral (reel) which is then placed in the tank. Most tanks allow processing in normal lighting, once the photographic material has been loaded into the tank which must be in total darkness.

Diffusion enlarger An enlarger which illuminates the negative (or transparency) with diffuse illumination, as opposed to condenser enlargers which pass more directional light through the negative. Diffusion enlargers produce images of slightly lower contrast and sharpness; when printing with black-and-white the contrast can be increased by the use of higher contrast papers. The effect of any scratches or other marks on the negative is minimized when a diffusion enlarger is used.

DIN Deutsche Industrie Norm. A film speed system used by Germany and some European countries. An increase, decrease of 3 DIN units indicates a doubling/halving of film speed, that is film of 21 DIN (100 ASA) is half the speed of a 24 DIN (200 ASA) film, and double the speed of an 18 DIN (50 AS film.

Dodging The technique used during enlarging which reduces exposure in certain parts of the image by blocking the light. A dodging tool is moved gently above those areas of the picture which require lightening (or darkening if printing from a transparency) while the remainder of the image receives the full exposure.

Drying marks Marks sometimes form while the processed film is drying; the may show up on the final print. Usuall drying marks are located on the film base side and are normally removed b careful rewashing or gentle rubbing with methylated spirit or a proprietary film cleaner. To avoid drying marks use a wetting agent in the final rinse and ensure that the water is clean.

E

Easel Also known as an enlarging eas or a masking frame. It holds the photographic paper flat while an enlarged image is projected on to it. Th easel also controls the size and squareness of the print borders.

Emulsion A photographic emulsion is the light-sensitive layer (or layers) which is coated on to the film or pape base. It consists of silver halide salts suspended in gelatin.

Emulsion speed See *ASA, ISO* and *D*

Enlargement This usually refers to a print (positive) made from a smaller negative (or transparency).

Enlarger A device which projects an image, usually of greater size than the original, negative or transparency, on photographic paper or film. Enlargers consist essentially of a light source, condenser(s) to control the light, a negative (transparency) holder, an enlarging lens, and some method of varying the negative-to-lens and lens-t paper distances.

Enlarging lens A lens which is specia

...signed to give excellent results at the ...atively short lens-to-paper distances ...ed in enlarging. A good enlarging lens ...essential for high quality prints.

...posure The result of allowing light to ...t on a photosensitive material. The ...ount of exposure depends on both ...e intensity of the light and the time it ...allowed to fall on the sensitive ...aterial.

...posure latitude The maximum ...riation of film or paper exposure from ...e 'correct' exposure which still yields ...ceptable results. For example, most ...our negative films have an exposure ...itude of -1 (one stop under) to +2 ...vo stops over). Exposure latitude ...bends on the actual film in use, ...ocessing, the subject and its lighting, ...d what is considered as acceptable to ...e photographer.

...rmer's reducer A solution of sodium ...osulphate (hypo) and potassium ...ricyanide that is used to lighten the ...ole or parts of a black-and-white ...nt or negative. The two chemicals are ...xed just prior to use. It is essential to ...t the effect of Farmer's reducer on a ...are print before applying to 'good' ...nts.

...st films Films that are very sensitive ...ight and require only a small ...osure. They are ideal for photo-...phy in dimly lit places, or ...ere fast shutter speeds (for example, ...00) and/or small apertures (for ...mple, f16) are required. These fast ...ns (400 ASA or more) are more ...iny than slower films.

...m speed See ASA, ISO and DIN.

...ter Any material which, when placed ...ront of a light source or lens, absorbs ...ne of the light coming through it. ...ers are usually made of glass, plastic, ...gelatin-coated plastic and in photo-...phy are mainly used to modify the light ...ching the film, or in colour printing ...hange the colour of the light reaching ...paper.

...egrain developer Any developer ...ich produces a relatively finegrained ...gative—usually this is accomplished ...hout the loss of film speed. Most ...dern developers are of the finegrain ...e—for example, D-76, ID-11, Acutol.

...er Solution which makes a ...otographic image permanent by ...solving all the remaining light ...sitive silver halides. Most fixers ...ntain a fixing agent (usually sodium ...ammonium thiosulphate), an acid, ...d a hardening agent to toughen the ...ocessed emulsion.

...gging The act, usually accidental, of ...or some parts of the photographic ...terial being developed as a result of ...mething other than exposure to the ...age. Fogging can be caused by light ...ks, chemical contaminants, radiation, ...tic discharges, and mechanical ...ess.

...aze A glossy surface that results ...en certain fibre-based printing ...oers are dried face-down on a glazing ...te or ferrotype plate.

Glossy paper A photographic paper surface that is ultra smooth and produced the greatest range of tones from white to a deep black—other paper surfaces produce a less dense black. Glossy colour papers produce not only the largest tonal range of paper surfaces but also the purest (most saturated) colours. A glossy surface is obtained automatically from resin-coated (RC) papers, but 'conventional' papers need to be glazed to obtain a high gloss.

Grain The random pattern within the photographic emulsion that is made up of the final (processed) metallic silver image. The grain pattern depends on the film emulsion, plus the type and degree of development.

H

Hardener chemical that causes a photographic emulsion to dry hard and be therefore less susceptible to damage from scratching. Hardeners are usually incorporated into fixing solutions.

I

Intensification The technique of adding density and/or contrast to an existing black-and-white negative which is too light to produce satisfactory prints. Chemical intensifiers cannot produce detail where none originally existed, but they can 'rescue' an otherwise unprintable negative.

ISO International Standards Organization The ISO number indicates the film speed and aims to replace the dual ASA and DIN systems. For example, a film rating of ASA 100, 21 DIN becomes ISO 100/21°.

L

Latent image The invisible image, produced by exposure of photographic film or paper to light, which is made visible by development. The latent image, when kept at low temperature and low humidity, can remain relatively stable for months and even years.

Latitude When used in connection with films, latitude refers to the amount of under- and over-exposure permissible to achieve acceptable images. Exposure latitude depends on type of film, subject, lighting and the visual quality of the final result. Colour materials, especially slide films, generally have less latitude than black-and-white films.

Light-tight Any container, room etc., which is not penetrated by light. In photography it is essential that developing tanks, changing bags, cameras and darkrooms are light-tight.

M

Mask Any device which obscures or modifies selectively one part of an image. Masks are used to alter the tonal scale, colour or content.

Monochrome A monochrome picture is the one which has only one colour; the term is normally applied to black-and-white prints or slides.

N

Negative carrier The unit which holds the negative (or slide) in the correct position between the enlarger light source and the enlarging lens.

O

Over-development Development which is longer than the recommended time. Over-development causes increase in contrast, graininess and fog level, and a loss in sharpness. Occasionally over-development can be used to good advantage when lighting is dim (see Push processing).

Over-exposure Exposure which is much more than the 'normal' or 'correct' exposure for the film or paper being used. Over-exposure can cause loss of highlight detail and reduction of image quality. See also Pull processing.

P

Printing frame A frame used in contact printing to hold the negative and photographic paper in contact while the exposure is made.

Pull processing A slang term which means to underdevelop a film or paper intentionally. This technique is used when films are over-exposed.

R

Rapid fixer A fast-acting fixing solution. Most rapid fixers use ammonium thiosulphate as the fixing agent.

Reducer A photographic reducer is used to decrease the density of a negative or print. There are a number of formulations, one of the most popular being Farmer's Reducer.

Replenisher A solution which is added in small quantities to a processing solution to keep it up to strength.

Resin-coated paper Photographic paper which has a plastic coating on either side of the paper base, the emulsion being coated on top of the plastic layer. RC papers are more convenient to process and dry than conventional papers but have poorer long-term keeping properties.

Reticulation A 'cracking' of the photographic emulsion which occurs when it receives a temperature shock (for example, hot developer in a very cold rinse).

Retouching The addition to, or removal of, parts of the image. This can simply be the repairing of slight blemishes (dust or hair lines) or complex airbrushing to alter the image completely. It is possible to retouch negatives or positives, in either black-and-white or colour.

S

Safelight A coloured light which does not fog the photographic material being used. For example, a yellow-orange safelight does not emit blue light, and is therefore suitable when working with materials sensitive only to blue light (e.g. most enlarging papers).

Shading See Dodging.

Silver halides The group of light-sensitive compounds used in photographic emulsions. Silver chloride and silver bromide are used in papers; silver bromide and silver iodide are used in films.

Soft-working developer Any developer which produces lower contrast than a 'normal' developer. It is useful when photographing very contrasty subjects.

Stock solution Any solution which can be stored and used as needed in small quantities. Many stock solutions are either diluted or mixed with another solution(s) just prior to use.

Stop bath A solution used to terminate the action of a developer. A stop bath is weakly acidic to counteract the alkalinity of the developer.

T

Test strip A series of different exposures on one sheet of paper or film to help determine the correct exposure.

Tonal range The comparison between intermediate tones of a print or scene, and the difference between the whitest and blackest extremes.

Toner Any chemical or set of chemicals which alter the colour of a black-and-white image.

Tungsten light A light source which produces light by passing electricity through a tungsten wire. Most domestic and much studio lighting uses tungsten lamps.

U

Under-development Less-than-normal development for a film or paper. This can be caused by low temperature, short development time, insufficient agitation, or exhausted developer.

Under-exposure An exposure which is less than the film or paper needs to give a 'normal' reproduction of the scene. See Push Processing.

Universal developer Any developer formulation which can be used for both film and paper processing, usually employed at different dilutions for each.

Uprating a film See Push processing.

V

Variable-contrast paper A black-and-white printing paper which has a range of contrasts depending on the colour of the filter used when enlarging. One box of variable-contrast paper replaces several boxes of different grades.

Vignetting The masking of the edges of an image. This can occur when a lens hood or filter intrudes into the subject area, or when a negative is enlarged through a shaped cut-out.

W

Wetting agent A chemical which is often added to the final processing rinse to promote even drying, thus avoiding drying marks.

Index

Artwork credits

Drury Lane 10-13, 31, 43, 52-87
Kevin Madison 28-9
John Thompson/Kevin Maddison 26 (bottom), 27
Peter Sullivan 19, 47-9
Technical Art Services 6-7
John Wells 26 (top)

Editorial credits

The Consultant Editor Neville Maude is an
industrial chemist by training who now has over
thirty years experience on the photographic scene.
He has written for all the major photographic
magazines, worked on television and radio, and is
currently a Consultant Editor for *The British
Journal of Photography* with special responsibility
for films, developers and darkroom work, and is
Editor of the specialist magazine, *The Photographic
Processor*.

Contributors: John Flack, David Hodgson,
Alan Jackson, David Kilpatrick, Kevin MacDonnell,
Neville Maude, Alan Meek, David Nicholson,
David Reed, Derek Watkins

Photographic credits

Stephen Ballantyne/Eaglemoss 66(bottom left and
right)
Steve Bicknell/Eaglemoss 20,23,68,86,89(top
left)
Tony Boxall 42
Michael Busselle/Eaglemoss 44-5
Bill Colman 30(bottom)
Tim Cook 79
Eric Crichton/Eaglemoss 81(top row)
John Garrett 32
Ilford Ltd 62,63,64
Pierre Jaffeux 84(right),85
David Kilpatrick/Eaglemoss 18,60
Barry Lewis 69-73
Barry Lewis/Eaglemoss 8-9, 34-41, 75
Philippa Longley 58(bottom left), 59(bottom
right)
Lisa Mackson 65

Naru/printed by Adrian Ensor 95
David Nicholson/Eaglemoss 78
Alasdair Ogilvie/Eaglemoss 51
Frank Owen/Eaglemoss 56-59
Paterson Products Ltd 74
Ricardo Gomez Perez 81 (middle and bottom rows)
David Pratt/Eaglemoss 87-8, 89(bottom)
Graham Pritchard 84(top and bottom left)
Con Putbrace/Eaglemoss 7,25,47,49,50
David Reed 77
Anthea Sieveking/ZEFA 30(top right)
John Swannell 61,67
Jack Taylor 82,83
Jack Taylor/Eaglemoss 90,91
Tony Timmington 54
Alison Trapmore/Eaglemoss 52,55
Malcolm Warrington/Eaglemoss 14-7,22,62(top
left),94

Cover: Allan Grainger (equipment
courtesy of Johnsons of Hendon)
Page 4: Jeanloup Sieff